Late in an Angler's Life

That other salmon, 1956.

Late in an Angler's Life
essays on the sport

Gordon M. Wickstrom
drawings by John Betts

embracing
The Life Lived in Fishing the Fly

with observations on
Its Theory and History

studying
Its Sensational Development in Late Modern Life

including
Angling Tales

and
Notes on Tackle, Past and Present

considering the question
Why We Fish

UNIVERSITY OF NEW MEXICO PRESS ∽ ALBUQUERQUE

LIBRARY OF CONGRESS CATALOGING-IN-PUBLICATION DATA

Wickstrom, Gordon M., 1926–
Late in an angler's life : essays on the sport /
Gordon M. Wickstrom.
p.   cm.
Includes bibliographical references.
ISBN 0-8263-3266-8 (cloth : alk. paper)
1. Fishing. 2. Fly fishing. I. Title.
SH441.W565 2004
799.12´4—dc22

2003028312

illustrations: John Betts unless otherwise noted
Book design and typography: Kathleen Sparkes
Body Type: Minion 11.5/15
Display Type: Mona Lisa

For Betty Smith Wickstrom

∾

Over half a century

Dear Companion of Heart, Mind, and Stream
making things possible and worth the doing

Betty and that other salmon, 1956.

Contents

∿

THE GUILD

Every Where in Every Time
There Work
The Whole and Ancient Company of Anglers,
The Order of the Desperate,
Who Let Down Nets and Lines to Fish,
From the Bottom to the Top,
From the Beginning to the End.
Let Me Be Counted in That Number!

⌐ GMW

Induction

IT IS ALWAYS LATER THAN WE THINK. Even when it is early, it's getting later, always later in the angler's life. But we hope, as we approach that *defining lateness,* that things will make more sense, become more vivid, and their values, clearer and clearer. The poet Wordsworth called it "years that bring the philosophic mind," the compensating virtue of old age.

And so the temptation is irresistible to bring that old angler's "philosophic" bent of mind to his fishing, which appears, interestingly enough, always to need fresh analysis, definition, and evaluation.

I hope that this book can accomplish some of that definition, analysis, and evaluation and do its subject some small honor in the process—before it's too late. The book is built of essays, longer and shorter, and a number of just notes, many of them having appeared first in my quarterly gazette:

The Bouldercreek Angler
a gazette for those who fish
〜

Gordon M. Wickstrom
editor and publisher
The Best Fishing Begins and Ends with an Idea.

The gazette's motto: "The best fishing begins and ends with an idea," controls the book, which becomes the account of one fisherman's lifelong wrangling with his sport, *of fishing through time* and its protean challenges and pleasures—but most of all, stewing around in its *ideas*—and always looking up ahead for good water into which to chuck his flies and find ideas.

I can claim nothing more than to have been on the creek most of my life, both in spirit and in truth. I have seen the water rise up and go down—and have thought about the experience. And I have surely enjoyed writing about it.

You, gentle reader, however you fish, must, if you can, find something of your own image and experience in mine, maybe even a bit of entertainment. I hope that we can be friends or, as Izaak Walton would have it, "brothers of the angle."

Perhaps these essays in angling criticism will find a tiny corner of their own in the great tradition of angling and its literature—each one, a step toward the *completion of the angler* that Walton envisioned in his great work. Let them be thought of as moments in the *contemplative man's recreation.*

Notice

WE SNEAKED INTO THE THIRD MILLENNIUM with scarcely a hurt, breathing a sigh of relief and feeling quite secure again. But who could know what was awaiting us some twenty-one months ahead into the third millennium. It happened! We felt badly broken and thought we would never be the same again.

Some of us thought we might possibly be shocked into a transformation of the national life. We thought we might leave behind much of the trash of our twentieth-century, pre–September 11 lives and paradoxically be enriched in a deeper, more humane, and generous future.

Some of us now feel that we have automatically neutralized those terrible days and weeks and have emerged on the other side much as we were before. The disappointment has been palpable. But that disappointment has now darkened into danger. Now we find ourselves changed as a nation in ways we could not have imagined. We live in daily dangers from others and even worse dangers from ourselves.

Nothing can escape the awfulness of this turn of the century and of the millennium. Nothing remains untouched: not even *fishing*.

And so it seems necessary to begin this collection of writings on fishing with three, perhaps four essays that, in their moment, dealt with just this immensity of events, facing up to it and placing us and our fishing within the sweep of these dangerous times.

↫ GMW

December 1999

"So hallowed and so gracious is the time...."

A dozen months, a dozen flies, a dozen fish,
a dozen of this and a dozen of that. Divisible in
twos and threes, fours and sixes—oh, mysterious,
powerful, wonderful number twelve of our lives!

IN *HAMLET*, MARCELLUS STANDS HIS FREEZING WATCH and, hearing the cock crow, speaks poignantly of the coming of that December season—"so hallowed and so gracious is the time." The twelfth month, for all its darkness and potential for despair, is the most sumptuous, the richest, most hallowed and gracious of all the months. We search its darkness with the brightly colored lights of Advent as though making light were our particular human responsibility. We know that it can't get any darker than December and that if we can just hang on and survive one more time, light and life will return.

This particular December of 1999 is charged with ending the second millennium, during which we went on trying to make something of ourselves, accomplishing wonders while inventing horrors never before imagined.

Now at the end, we need the rest and restoration that December traditionally offers—in order to brace ourselves in the presence of the great void looming out there, ominous and demanding to be filled with still more and more of our troubled experience of ourselves.

Maybe fish need that rest and restoration too.... Maybe all creatures do....

In the old days the Colorado fishing season ended abruptly on Halloween. We put away our tackle with various degrees of ceremony until once again in December, the solstice would work its way down deep into our genes, getting us restless and thinking of spring. We lusted for holiday gifts of swell new tackle. The long nights found us opening our vests like reliquaries and tinkering away, reading books and catalogs, fantasizing what the next season might bring.

If structure in our lives is a good thing, the structure of limited fishing seasons once gave articulate shape to the angling year. We gave the trout a rest, allowing brown and brook to spawn in peace and rainbow and cutthroat time to enjoy the anticipation of it.

Perhaps it would be a good thing if we stopped fishing during December, a brief hiatus in our pursuit of pleasure. December lore suggests the sanctity of all critters and the possibility that, when in Marcellus's words "the nights are wholesome," and we listen carefully, there can be communion between them and us—a Peaceable Kingdom, a spell of grace before the next big push into we know not what.

RIO PUEBLO DE TAOS

Flowing through the center of Taos Pueblo is a small stream, the puebloans' single water supply. They bucket it directly to their homes. It is also a trout stream. For most of a thousand years these people have lived in their adobe apartments close up against sacred Taos Mountain, down which the stream flows to them.

They say they have never allowed human beings to live or keep their sheep upstream on the mountain. Above the pueblo all is pristine. In return for this protection of their mountain, the gods send down to the people the dearest of all good gifts: pure water.

Of Girlfriends, Grasshoppers, and New York

*On the 11th of September they tried to
kill my children and my country.*

IT HAD TO HAVE BEEN BACK IN 1946, when one day my girlfriend
to-be-wife and I went over to fish the Saint Vrain below Lyons,
Colorado. Along this couple miles of stream are several irriga-
tion diversions and weirs into which trout get shunted off.

Anyway, on this day, we pulled off to park near one of those
concrete diversions, and, as we were gearing up, noticed two old
men in farmers' overalls sitting on the high concrete rim of the
diversion, fishing away with what we were to learn were live
grasshoppers—of which each had a jar full. If you ever saw two
farmers, as opposed to city folk, they were these two happy old
men, obviously come from out in the valley up into the foothills.

And they had a pile of hefty brown trout on the grass—well
on their way to a twenty-five-a-day fish limit. Betty and I stopped
to admire their fish and maybe learn something. They in turn were
full of good cheer, especially for Betty, but were not about to tell
me how they were working their grasshoppers off their old fly rods
with such success.

Smiling from ear to ear, one of the old gents in blue said, "Little lady, would you like to catch a fish? Come on, we'll show you how." Betty was eager enough. And I got told to clear out, disappear, on down the creek. I was *not* invited. Okay, I thought, I'd better do as I was told and disappeared downstream, working a Black Ghost streamer I'd just tied, jungle cock and all, to nary a sign of a fish—for most of an hour.

Thinking: Enough of this! I went back to the diversion, where Betty was sitting happily between the two old codgers, with two or three browns of her own on the grass. I got cheerfully laughed at for my failure and for her success. What the hell good is a boyfriend who can't help his girl get a mess of fish! Such is the romance of angling!

Furthermore, there's hardly anything in nature to match the slash of a brown trout at a live and kicking floating grasshopper.

But my point is this: Times have changed. Back then, there was a real *democracy* on our streams—a place for us all to fish side by side with everything from dry flies to sucker meat. I can't remember that anyone would have challenged anyone else's right or rightness to fish in any old way.

That has changed radically. The fly-fishing community has taken over and purged the creeks of farmers' overalls and grasshoppers. Many pay guides to help them establish and hold what they have come to believe are their territorial rights even on public water.

Now that I'm a bona fide "old codger" myself, I believe that it's too late for such exclusivity, that it's a bad way to fish. I wish we could go back to that older democratic, shared use of our fish and the water, though I know well enough that we can never really "go back" to anything. But still we are right to yearn for those aspects of our past that helped us sustain a good life. The quality of our present lives is as much determined by what we desire from life as what we think we, in fact, are. The model for that older way of which I dream is Betty's and my experience with those two good old men and their grasshoppers.

The pretension to superiority and privilege among fly fishers over the rest of fishermen and fisherwomen just will not do any longer. I understand the claim of fly fishing to special privilege. The fly fisher can rightly claim to injure fewer fish and so release them with a better chance of their survival. Tying flies is also easier than digging worms in our urban situation. Casting flies is an elegant thing to do—all of it marvelously *visual*. And the flies themselves are certainly fascinating in their own right for us casual students of life and sport.

In the last analysis, though, no artificial fly can ever be as fascinating as is a living grasshopper, worm, or minnow to the serious student of living things. When I first took my granddaughter fishing, she understood clearly how much more interesting and important was the wiggling worm in her hand than the lifeless flies in my boxes. *And a little child shall lead them.*

To New York? How do I get there? I write this exactly one week after the calamity of September 11, about that heroic city where great numbers of lovely native brook trout once lived and loved their worms. It seems to me now that we are so hugely indebted to New York for bearing our national anguish that we have to toughen up and, in the strength of the virtues of which we as a people are certain, be prepared for action at once hard as nails and tender as the heart. How shall we know when to be hard and when to be tender? Knowing will always be difficult. But we can't allow our effort *to try to know* to be further compromised by the *slop* of our turn-of-the-millennium national life. We need to renew our way of being American people, adding to it a new rigor of freedom and fellowship. We must be better than we were before.

Anglers? Well, we anglers might just as well begin our own reconstruction out on our streams, in our moral blue overalls, and be worth our penny. In the meantime, we must not let the bastards get us! If they knew what a lovely thing we do out fishing, they would hate us all the more and even more violently.

After New York City on September 11, in the first full year of this new millennium, now that we know what it can do to us, we have almost to start over again. The great Irish poet William Butler Yeats wrote of where all ladders upward must begin—"in the foul rag and bone shop of the heart." That's where anglers, too, must start in order to find a way to fish up from the bottom.

Consider

Consider the presence of wild strains of geologically isolated brown trout in the headwaters of the Tigris and Euphrates rivers in the mountains of Turkey. Those strains had, they say, to have come up those rivers from the Persian Gulf when those waters were cooler.

Are we, therefore, entitled to believe that there were brown trout in *the Garden of Eden?* How about Baghdad today?

Saint Patrick's Day, 2003

If you have tears, prepare to shed them now.
—Mark Antony, *Julius Caesar*, Act III, scene ii

LAST THURSDAY: THERE I WAS ON THE SAINT VRAIN, a fine, springlike morning. I had been fishless over a dozen midging rainbows. So, I gave up. Nothing to do with the brand-new rod in my hand but give it a maiden tryout to see what it would really do when . . . on the power stroke of an experimental fifty footer, I heard and felt an ominous *snap* right under my hand. The rod had broken clean in two exactly in the middle of the grip!

This rod was a curious golden yellow little thing of retro fiberglass, seven feet long, light as air, and of six pieces for traveling convenience. The blanks had been hidden away somewhere as in a time capsule before they got to me from a friend who had got hold of four or more sets of them at the fly tackle dealers' show in Denver a couple of years ago. He all but gave me two sets of the sticks, from which I finished up one rod. Another good friend shamelessly letched for the rod until I ended up just giving it to him. Then, just lately, I did up the second set for myself. The resulting rod looked nifty with deep maroon wraps on the golden glass.

But on that trial long cast on the Saint Vrain it broke in my hand, all its strength, like Samson's, suddenly drained completely away. Sickening. Who the hell ever broke a rod in the grip right under his hand!

So, I headed home, but not before stopping in Lyons at The Soda Fountain to see if one of their lavish chocolate malts might make me feel better, which it did—a little—when sprinkled with nutmeg.

Then too, right across the street from The Soda Fountain is master cane rod maker Mike Clark's classy studio-shop. I thought I'd give Mike a chance to offer his comfort for my loss. He offered no comfort at all but rather rubbed it in a bit, calling attention to the folly of my fooling around with glass at my time of life. He offered the philosophic view that I ought to have known better and how, since I had not, I might just as well take my medicine like a man.

And so I drove home, only to find e-mail from clear across this unhappy nation, from the American Museum of Fly Fishing in Vermont, to the effect that in the hot-off-the-press issue of *The Bouldercreek Angler,* I had made the most egregious error, the wrong goddamned word in the worst possible place—which I shall not, will not, dear reader, identify for you. Find it for yourself! (If you haven't already... in vol. 5, no. 1, March 2003.) The museum, suffice it to say, was in transports of glee at my expense.

Anyhow, I could at least look forward to the evening and dinner with good old friends. Maybe they would help me "to grieve" as do the professional grief masters who rush in to scavenge on any and every disaster.... But I ought to have known that they wouldn't really care much about my poor rod. And besides, we'd probably spend most of the evening pouring ashes over our heads as we looked forward to the advent of our presidential war.

Finally then, and looking back on that cheerless Saint Patrick's day, I wish to all bloody hell that things in this world were no worse than the breaking of a brand-new, pretty little golden glass fly rod—even after having gone fishless on the first fishing day of the new year.

And Yet Another Break—In a Broken World

I did it again: broke another rod. But this time it was no bit of golden glass but a one-of-a-kind, five-strip cane stick built in 1948 by that distinguished theoretician, rod builder, and inventor of the supremely important Super Z ferrule Louis B. Feierabend.*

I got the rod from Lou in 1949. It's two piece, eight feet long, and built on a 14/64-inch ferrule and a 5/64-inch tip top—a strong but compliant, all-round fly rod if ever there was one— my very most favorite. Just imagine how many casts it had made over its fifty-four years of hard use—before it broke cleanly in two, right at the point in the butt section where the ferrule serrations terminate and meet the unsupported cane!

Mike Clark points out how difficult it is to prevent the varnish on the wrapping at that point where metal meets wood from cracking and letting in moisture that never quite dries out, especially over five decades. Rot sets in, and eventually the rod, on a fateful forward cast, may just plain break in two.

On my fateful day, my fishing companion Lee Devin offered me the use of his extra rod. But I couldn't bring myself to use it. Seems to me that in these dire times, we need to remain faithful to what we can, where we can. I want to keep faith with my old tackle. So, on that day it seemed appropriate for me just to quit fishing in honor of that dear broken rod.†

*Lou lives in retirement in Grand Junction, Colorado.
†Mike Clark has fixed it. How many more casts are there in it?

Fortune-telling

WHEN IN EARLY 1999, I HAD THE EFFRONTERY TO LAUNCH *The Bouldercreek Angler* on the unsuspecting, we were all looking ahead with considerable trepidation to the arrival of the next century and the third millennium. Many feared Y2K, the breakdown of all cybernetic technology and the collapse of the civilized world. Others, of religious enthusiasms, looked forward to the Apocalypse and the coming Judgment, as had their forebears at the turn of the second millennium, AD 999.

Like those forebears, everyone in *our* own triple nine was running for cover of one kind or other. Then, lo and behold, on the stroke of midnight New Year's Eve/Day, the computers of the world held. The heavens did not open to receive in rapture the religious. It appeared that we had got away scot-free (little did we know…) with the sins of that awful twentieth century. For about twenty-one months, that is, and you know the rest of the terrible story.

Anyhow, back in that early spring of 1999, in the second issue of the *Bouldercreek Angler,* I thought I would look ahead to what our fishing might be like in the next century and so went out on the dangerous limb of predicting the future.

I've just now looked at those ten predictions and find I still believe them. And so, in the spirit of looking on the dark side of things, here they are again—to worry about.

1. Demographic changes will favor those with little or no tradition of field sports and will result in comparatively fewer anglers. Those remaining will have less political and economic influence.

2. Disease among the fishes, and in their environment, will continue and probably worsen.

3. Open access to selected great trout and salmon rivers may end, with days on public water controlled by public lottery.

4. Some great public water systems may be closed to fishing permanently and entirely. Yellowstone Park has been mentioned.

5. Animal rights organizations will disrupt and make greater inroads on fishing and its rights.

6. Problems of legal water rights and ownership will become more difficult and frustrating. Urban and industrial water needs will defeat angling needs.

7. Privatization of fishing and outsized land ownership will increase steadily, making it more difficult and increasingly expensive to fish. Casual, local, frequent fishing will diminish.

8. There will necessarily be less emphasis on trout and salmon. Warm-water and reservoir fisheries will become more and more important.

9. Fishing in distant, exotic waters will become increasingly attractive, the hegemony of Britain, Ireland, and North America having ended.

10. Virtual, cybernetic substitutes for angling will increase in volume, variety, and sophistication. Direct experience of anything will be thought less and less essential.

WHAT TO BE WARY OF ON THE STREAM
dogs
cell phones
caps on backward
guides
falling down and in
naked and seminaked anglers
lightning

In Autumn Leaves

WE LIVED UP ON FIFTH STREET, CLOSE TO THE MOUNTAINS and near the creek, a fine neighborhood for kids—half of it still in vacant lots where, on fine evenings after supper, we ganged up to run our games.

When I was fourteen, the Douglas family moved in next door with their two kids, a son my age and his younger sister—a dream of a younger sister!

Those were years of turbulent discovery of ourselves, each other, and the world—all heavy with desire. I had discovered and grown obsessed with the trout in the creek, and now here was that girl next door! I hardly knew how or which way to turn.

On this far side of life, I see that for a boy as besotted as I, trout and girl were much alike—both uncatchable—a dual fantasy of desire unfulfilled, ever alluring and inviting.

One autumn night, playing our games in those vacant lots and streets, I caught a glimpse of that stick-slender, black-haired, happy-eyed girl next door running behind me. There was just a possibility that . . . if I'd drop down in the leaves between those old maples there at Fourth and Pearl and pretend to be knocked out, badly injured, or something like that, she'd find me and be frightened and so very sorry—and drop to her knees and love me! Surely she would!

So down I went among the acrid leaves to lie motionless, one eye squinting up to see her coming, find me lying there, blithely look the other way, and run on—leaving me alone and desolate.

I could no more lure that girl with my kid's love than I could those trout in the creek with my crudely tied flies. I could only watch and yearn as they disappeared into their ancient, mysterious elements.

Most Interesting

Wishing always to provide my students with good counsel, I advised them that in my view, the most interesting things under the sun were *religion, art, politics, sex,* and *fishing*—though not in any necessary order of preference or importance. They were always amused, not yet able to recognize the seriousness of having to make such crucial alignments in their lives.

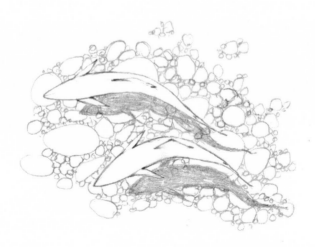

A Silhouette

I OFTEN THINK THAT LIFE IS NOT SO MUCH, as they say, a process of "growing up" or "maturing" as it is putting in the necessary time in which to *come to our senses.* The time may be short or long as the experience requires, but it does take its own sweet *time.*

It struck me, when explaining to students the difference between tragedy and comedy, that the secret of comedy on the stage is not so much the demonstration of a worked-out *solution* to the desperate problems in which the characters find themselves as it is just putting in the necessary time, suffering the problem in symbolic stage time, until they *come to their senses* about it and declare their troubles to have become successes after all. We just "snap out of it."

It took me half a century to come to my senses about a fishing picture for which I used to have only disdain and wondered why I kept it, but which now I value so highly. Today it is a central icon in whatever fishing has come to mean to me.

Here's the story. During the Great Depression, there were lots of homemade Christmas gifts. My aunt Minnie Rossman,* having got her share of the family genes for graphic art, for the Christmas of 1936 made each of us small nephews and nieces a silhouette painting of the sort much in vogue at the time.

Silhouette, by Minnie Rossman, 1934.

Aunt Minnie painted in solid black on a nine-by-eleven-inch sheet of glass a silhouette of a boy and his dog sitting under an overhanging tree on a high grassy bank still-fishing in the water below. The boy holds what must be a cane pole, his line disappearing out into space, the vast space in which his bobber floats.

The trick of these silhouette paintings was to back the painted glass with some special paper. In the case of my painting, the background is a Christmas gift-wrapping paper, a beautiful metallic silver paper with embossed bursting stars of light. My angler boy appears to be fishing off into the very vastness of space itself—the sort of "sea of crystal light" into which the fishermen three—Wynken, Blynken, and Nod—sailed off in their wooden shoe, in that wondrous lullaby of a poem, to fish for the stars, "to fish for the herring fish that live in this beautiful sea."†

Now, I have trouble where the company of a dog on fishing trips is concerned. I think they should stay home, but I tolerate *this* Scottie-looking mutt whose concentration on the bobber is just as intense as is the boy's. Their total, timeless concentration is deeply moving. But it's that *bobber* floating in the limitless space of the stars that obsesses me. The bobber is suspended in two worlds simultaneously: in air and water, in our world and in the fishes'.

I've written that whatever else fishing is, essential is the problem of getting through the surface of the water into that mysterious, even forbidden otherworld of the fishes. Aunt Minnie's silhouette does just that. *Pisces in the skies.*

The way the boy's line goes out and down into watery space is matchlessly realized. The angling technique is transparent, though the mystery of it remains opaque. It is all so beautiful and evocative for me now, this 1930s Depression silhouette that once meant almost nothing to me. Now it's become a central metaphor in the life of a boy turned into an old man trying to find his way through surfaces.

How could I get along now without this image-idea? What if I had discarded it!

---

*In the first essay in my previous *Notes from an Old Fly Book,* I wrote how it was Aunt Minnie, some half-dozen years later, when her husband, my uncle Clarence, died, who gave me all his fishing tackle, including his Granger fly rod. Someone has said that there is only one story to be told and that is of family.

†Eugene Field, *Wynken, Blynken, and Nod* (New York: North-South Books, 1995).

Kids Learning to Fish
A Mentor's Plan • *Principles*
The mentor should have a long-term, sustained relationship
 with the kid.
The kid should not be recruited to fish but come to
 it voluntarily, "naturally."
The kid should be between twelve and fourteen years old.
Instruction should be one-on-one, avoiding anything
 suggesting the classroom.
Remember: kids distract other kids.
Instruction should be regular and repeated on the same
 friendly stream.
Work to prevent buildup of frustration, the kid's or
 the mentor's.
Do not require success! Be ready and willing to give it up.
Avoid waters set aside just for kids. No "kiddie ponds."
Keep in mind that the purpose of this instruction is for
 the kid to learn to *fish* and only in the processes of
 that to learn to fish the fly.

Process
Introduction to the IDEA of fishing.
Introduction to the hand line. Use it with live bait on panfish.
Introduction to the fly rod as a general-purpose rod.
 Use live bait, spinners, and spinner-flies on panfish.
Move from lake or pond to stream.
Introduction to the FLY and fly casting. Problem of
 terminal tackle: knots.
Acquire basic equipment. Visit big general fishing
 tackle stores, then fly shops.
Encourage collection and study of tackle catalogs
 and magazines.

Introduction to the trout and its world.
Introduction to stream craft.
Discuss killing and not killing fish.
Discuss fishing ethics.
Introduce the kid to older, experienced anglers.
Send the kid out to fish alone and get back a report.
Finally, and only when the above are well "set," discuss
    the principle and proper use of spinning tackle,
    the use of "hardware."
Do NOT allow use of cheap enclosed spool reels.

Note: Do not encourage fly tying until it is clear that the kid is
    a confirmed, if as yet young and inexperienced, angler.
This plan can readily be adapted to a kid and bass fishing.
Make any changes necessary in the above plan in order to
    make it successful.

The New Adventurers and Me

AT THE KITCHEN TABLE ONE MORNING I COMPLAINED to Betty that I couldn't come up with an entry for the year AD 2000 for the second and "Millennial" edition of my *Chronology of Fly Fishing*—a thirty-nine-inch graphic display of fly fishing's 504 years since the great *Treatyse* in the *Boke of Saint Albans* of 1496.

Betty stood listening to my problem, all the while with the morning mail in her hand. Having heard me out, she began sorting through the mail and turned up the new 1999 Dan Bailey catalog from Montana, showing on its cover John Bailey astride an elephant in a river in India casting his flies for the supershy mahseer. He even has a guide running the elephant, if that's what they do with elephants. . . .

Bang! I had it! The *internationalization of fly fishing:* its *globalization,* the end, at last, of the hegemony of the British Isles, Ireland, and North America. A new breed of serious, vigorous adventurer-anglers were catching planes to Mongolia, Russia, Africa, and Argentina, to say nothing of Alaska, eastern Europe, and Tasmania. Many sought the wild places for the sake of adventure as much as for fishing.

And so my entry for the year 2000 became:

*By century's end fly fishing had become global, no longer
the peculiar province of the British Isles and North America.
Anglers were now flying the world over to cast their flies to
myriad exotic fish. New tackle, techniques, traditions, and
literatures were developing everywhere in an expanding
universe of the artificial fishing fly.*

I felt as though I were authorizing a major transformation
in the sport, turning it over to a new generation determined to
make fishing its own. I sensed that they might be looking for a
new/old kind of *freedom,* the freedom of place and of going there
that the developed world has so circumscribed and limited. My
grandparents knew such freedom, a particularly American freedom, and lived according to its fortunes and losses, its insecu-
rities and exaltations. They died by it too. Perhaps, at bottom,
what the new fishing adventurers might be seeking is their
revenge on *modernity.*

Say what you will, though: I felt left out. I knew I was not to
play a part in this new dispensation. I am old and outdated.

If the new breed of anglers were to be world adventurers as
much as anglers, I was indeed left out. That spirit was not mine,
not part of my growing up in fishing. We are, most of us, it would
seem, pretty affluent these days, affluent beyond our expectations—particularly this new, younger generation. It has grown
up accepting as normal that they should pay for and afford their
sport. They are content that much of fishing and hunting should
be private and costly in one way or another. We holdovers from
olden times reflexively thought of our sport as public and free
and mostly close by. We would not have thought it quite right
to spend a lot of money on it. We kept our sport local and inex-
pensive. Ours was a point of view developed out of the Great
Depression and, just as important, out of the egalitarian social,
economic, and cultural theory and national experience that
attended it. We were New Dealers at heart.

With me there is also the age factor. I've written in other pages that one of the undoubted values of fishing is that one can do it into old age. Perhaps I overwrote that precept. Perhaps old age wears us down more surely than I expected ten years ago. I now feel myself stumbling around in the stream, fearing to fall down and seriously hurt myself. I haven't the general stamina to keep up with younger anglers. I worry about being a drag on them and so think up excuses to turn down their generous invitations to fish together. It gets easier and easier to keep to home and home waters.

In still other pages I wrote to predict the increase of the *virtual,* cybernetic experience of almost everything and fishing certainly. The computer will become more and more central in our lives. I thought I saw fishing on the Internet, on television, in magazines, in numberless new books, in richly appointed fly shops taking the place of the *real thing.* It was, perhaps, an old curmudgeon's point of view, of course. But now I'm suddenly brought up short with the realization that I've been carrying around with me all my life the most powerful of all engines of virtual experience: this *brain* of mine, in which I can live the richest life of the imagination, of its adventure out in the world and in its ideas in my head. The system is without limits. It's this brain of mine and this keyboard at my fingers' ends that promises me the longest-possible life in angling.

In other pages yet, I've written that fishing is the most "thinking about it" of all sports. It certainly is the most "writing about it" of them all. I'll wager that the thinking and writing that is done about fishing has had more to do with its development than all the 504 years of actual work on the water. Fishing is *the mind's adventure* regardless of airplanes, budgets, and travel agents.

I dream of those browns in the Tierra del Fuego. Photographs of them, those virtual records of their splendor, appease my mind's need for direct experience. Remember, when, at the turning into the nineteenth century, the poet Wordsworth had to explain all this, without the metaphor of the computer, he spoke of old age as "years that bring the philosophic mind."

In my "philosophy" I see, for instance, the new technologically advanced tackle of the new generation. I read stories of their rituals of adventure in the press. I stare in wonder at their photography that comes close to being as good as the real thing. I ruminate on the many new species of fish that will come to the fly in remote, even dangerous corners of the planet. How beautiful they must be, how infinite in their variety!

The language of geography, expressions like *Pacific Rim,* is deeply stirring. Just to think that *our* salmonids on this, our home side of the *Rim,* are *their* salmonids also, on their other side. It's a knockout of an idea: *the salmonids of Asia,* for God's sake! Marco Polo might have seen and eaten them. . . . Who would not, in his right mind and heart, want to go there and fish those treasures! I recall with a thankful vengeance that I have eaten that delicious little *aiu,* that strange little salmonid, in Japan, though the bony plates of its skull were hard for me to get down. You see, I have not been altogether a stay-at-home.

Then think of the trout in the Southern Hemisphere, where none were ever native, but where crazy English fishing adventurers took them nearly a century ago. Fly fishing has indeed gone global.

Who in his right angler's imagination would not want to find those several different breeds of brown trout in the mountains of northern Turkey or Macedonia? To say nothing of those in North Africa.

But I shan't go. My old way is dying out—as surely as are we old anglers, for whom the old way was the only way. I like to reflect on a powerful emblem of that old way that separates us quite from the new breed. That's our dear old tackle, so different from the new high-technology equipment trading these days between Siberia and Argentina.

The fly-fishing industry has invented and supplied altogether replaceable, interchangeable, impersonal tackle for which it is difficult to feel any affection. Break one carbon rod and there's always a new and identical one immediately to hand. But break my eight-foot, five strips of Tonkin cane and it's gone forever and ever and ever. The world would be diminished by its loss.

As I ponder this, I feel more and more the deep necessity of keeping faith with that rod and its accouterments. My old tackle is indeed emblematic, a system of wonderful relics, charged with the powers of the past and representative of my generation, what we did and who we were.

In the meantime, while I do my pondering, may the new adventurers travel bravely, fish hard, and return home safe and sound.

PERHAPS...

I have seen the "old folks" sitting in lawn chairs along the shores of lakes and reservoirs, quietly and contentedly and often successfully plying trout with bait tossed from spinning reels to good distances and, in the spirit of the forked stick, waiting patiently for a "bite."

Perhaps that's not too terrible a fate for old folks. Where they haunt, it's right and proper to kill a few fish for the table in the spirit of their old times. And if they have packed along really good lunches and are companionable, such fishing would most likely be right down enjoyable. Don't forget, these old folks always have lots to talk about and remember as they wile away the spells between bites. And after all, *fishing is fishing* in whatever its form and practice. I think I shall take heart from this and not despair after all.

A Portrait of the New Fly Fisher

THERE'S A NEW BREED OF FLY FISHER OUT THERE on the water, casting to a new beat of that same old yearning for the trout to come to the fly. It helps to understand this new breed if one can remember or, better still, have been one of that old gang of anglers who threw their flies down the decades before, let's say, 1960, after which the big change set in. It's worth pausing now to draw a portrait of that new angler as she wades into the third millennium. Let me try to depict her.

Male and female created He them, and to each He assigned their proper tasks. And so, until our own time, up until about 1960, men did the fishing and women stayed home and did the cooking. And that was that.

But now, *gender* has entered the field as a factor in fly fishing. Men and women are inextricably mixed on the stream and are confounding my very effort at a portrait by the difficulty that gender makes for our language. Old-timers will want to cling to the comforts of the old nomen "fisherman," even as it fails to acknowledge the great numbers of women who have taken to long rods with enthusiasm and skill. Women are leaving their mark on the sport in no uncertain terms, but writers don't know by what name to call them. What shall I write: *he* or *she? Fisherman* or just *fisher?* Does the equivocal term *fly fisher* cover all bets satisfactorily? For that matter, is this to be a portrait of a man or a woman?

∼

Where the fisherman of old tended to stay close to home waters, mastering them and in more than a few cases making those waters famous, the new fly fisher in our portrait ranges the world over in search of wild and infinitely various fish and adventure. Where Theodore Gordon stayed close to his Neversink in the Catskills and Vincent Marinaro to his Letort Spring Run, our new angler has comparatively little confidence or interest in local waters: Mongolia, Tierra del Fuego, and Africa are too powerful a lure, to say nothing of the closer fish-factory tailwaters created by the post–World War II reservoirs. The new angler, spending more of his income on his fishing than ever before, is commonly seen on airport concourses lugging rod tubes and duffels toward his plane to the remotest corners of the world.

I suspect that this venturing forth all over the place is underlain by a deep anxiety about what our angler feels is happening close to home, that his home waters are fast being urbanized out from under him. The irony that what supports his urban life and times is exactly that which is destroying his fishing may further contribute to his anxiety.

Shadow falls across the portrait.

∼

Many today try to keep in shape by working out on fantastic machines in the gym. Few, like the old-timers, stay tough by hard physical work on the job. We might therefore expect the new fly fisher to be a model of health and endurance. In any case, it's certain that this portrait ought to be suffused with energy and athletic drive.

❧

The new fly fisher commonly has a different relationship to her job than did anglers of the past, whose eight-hour day usually ended at five-thirty, with time left over to hit the evening rise on the local stream. No longer. The boomers are now working God knows how many hours with no time for anything but the job and guilt about their neglect of everything else. And most struggling families are driven by not one but two of these all-consuming, demanding jobs.

Their interest in fishing is intense but with less time to do it. Too often the year's fishing is crammed into one or two frantic vacation trips, nothing casual about it anymore. The image is one of haste and stress.

❧

In self-defense our fly fisher spends bits and pieces of salvaged time in *virtual* fishing. With the computer a part of his tackle, he works the Internet, watches videos, goes to fly-fishing shows, reads books and magazines, collects trout art—every imaginable substitute. Yes, he fishes deep into his imagination, where he has learned to find satisfaction. He has discovered that fishing is probably the most rewarding of all sports just to *think about* and talk about. It is as intellectually challenging as he cares to make it. It's also inexhaustible.

❧

Being at home in the *virtual* is but one of the uses of the new technology that permeates modern life and angling. In a technological culture, angling finds it place. While some might regret angling's submission to the satisfactions of technology, there appears to be no retreat. Note that it leaves not a single line of regret on the face of the angler in our portrait.

∾

But on closer inspection, there may be a few lines of regret after all. The new fly fisher may be uneasy about the future of his sport and look backward into the annals of fishing to find assurance and inspiration for the present. He tends to be more historically minded than his predecessors, as though *looking forward into the past* might reveal secrets of value ... for example, the spey rod and cast.

∾

This interest in the past extends to tackle making and innovation. There's more respect today for and interest in what the forebears did and how they did it. If they made rods of hickory and cast lines of horsehair and silk, why should we not explore what they did in the spirit of both honor to them and profit to us?

The result is that the new fly fisher knows more about tackle, ancient and modern, than anglers of the past. The new fly fisher is *smart.* (How does one draw *smart* into a portrait?)

∾

Then, too, schooled by excellent modern research and publication, she has become a capable student of aquatic insect life. (The entomology of most old-timers was painfully inadequate.)

One thing leads to another, and the new fly fisher is now one of a legion of fly tyers, most of them superbly skilled. In this golden age of fly tying, she knows her flies, alive and as imitation.

Her complex and detailed fly boxes, entomologically correct, would confound with amazement the older angler.

∽

But amid all this latter-day sophistication, there lies a serious lacuna, a crucial flaw, in the new fly fisher's intellectual equipment. She appears to know little and feel less for that barefoot boy of legend, with his willow pole and bobber, making his way down the country lane to the old fishing hole. Few grandfathers, indeed, go back far enough anymore to recall that elemental country fishing. The rural, country experience is no longer ours and is foreign, if not forgotten, in our new natures. For the new fisher, graphite has become as natural as willow and nylon as natural as gut. His tackle and its use have become the expression of *industry,* not of personal hand craftsmanship. His new tackle has lost all innocence and is almost brutally efficient.

∽

This new angler believes in experts and their instruction. There is little time for trial and error, lonely intuition, or the school of hard knocks in which to become a polished angler. He's in a hurry. Time is short, and he's willing to pay for shortcuts to competence and success. Most noticeably he turns to another new breed of angler, to professional *guides,* to help him fish.

∽

This portrait of the new fly fisher is interchangeable among anglers. One angler will look pretty much like another. His clothes, from waders, to vest, to hat, inside and out, have become more *costume* than clothing—they have been severely regularized and standardized by "the industry." *Sameness* is everywhere, with little or no room for the memorable eccentricities that we used to see and admire in many old-timers.

No creel is seen hanging on the fly fisher in this portrait. He has no interest in dead fish, having by now been thoroughly inculcated into releasing his catch. If getting food was once the raison d'être of all fishing, our new man or woman tends to assume that all food now comes, not from the field, but properly from the market. A trout belongs in the stream.

Still, he wants to catch as many and as big fish as he can. Where T. S. Eliot's nominal man of the twentieth century, J. Alfred Prufrock, "measured out [his] life in coffee spoons," our new angler measures out his in "twenty inchers." The portrait reveals a certain smallness about him, this competitive stress and compulsion for twenty inchers, though it's fair to say that increasingly anglers here and there are rejecting that compulsion and seeking out more intimate angling pleasures.

There's something else in the expression on the new angler's face. I think I see a new *tolerance* in his view of things. No longer does he spurn all fish but trout or salmon. He's discovered warm-water fishing and its undoubted rewards. He's eager to go after exotic fish of all kinds that may not have seen a fly before. He's more genuinely interested in fish for their own sake than were his predecessors. At the same time he's showing a more tolerant attitude toward a wider variety of fishing techniques. His mind plays more freely and actively over the entire *idea of fishing.* He is less and less dogmatic and more pragmatic, more "scientific."

Still, in his willingness to acknowledge and make the most of change, he hopes deep down that fishing will hang on as it has through the ages and resist changing at its *core.* If fishing must change, let it be at the edges.

A deepening gloom in the background of this portrait is the new fly fisher's *political* context. In a world where, like it or not, everything is deeply political, our fly fisher resists thinking of her angling as in any way politically determined. Politics too often feel nasty. Anglers nod to politics by a token membership in Trout Unlimited, itself prevented from effective political action by its contract with the devil IRS for its nonprofit status.

I want to suggest that another and deepening shadow on the portrait is our subject's scarcely conscious understanding that angling in its deepest nature is a *conservative* endeavor and impulse. Fishing is *elemental* in its meaning as food for the preservation of life. Fishing tends to be solitary, private, competitive, territorial, acquisitive, and traditional—all the ancient values of the true conservative.

On the other hand, this same conservative angler finds herself drawn to and feeling responsible for issues of the environment, for the health and welfare of fish and their waters everywhere. It's do or die to preserve them.

This work for preservation and nurture crosses lines of property, is accomplished only by social and political action, and is *public* in its values—and at the expense of the conservative values of property and privacy.

Our new fly fisher is being tossed on the horns of an awful dilemma, between the competing social-political issues of conservative and liberal ideologies. Too often he simply collapses in face of the complexity and contradictions of the dilemma, gives up on politics, and becomes passively complicit in the demise of his beloved fishing.

So there it is. Is this portrait complete? Is it finished? Not likely. Change is always on the way. We dare not, I think, be optimistic about changes on our horizon. At the same time, we hope for the best. Perhaps a new portrait will soon need to be drawn. We hope that we will be able to recognize the subject as the real thing, an even more accomplished and versatile fly fisher, male or female, with whom we'd like to go fishing.

The Creation

Ishi, the last of the Yani people of the foothills of Mount Lassen in California, told this tale of the creation of their *salmon world*.*

Grandfather said, "Back in the Olden Days, the Great Gods, Jupka and Kaltsuna, one day were fishing in the Outer Ocean. Jupka, throwing out a long line, which sank deep into the water, fished up the uncreated world from the ocean floor. It floated on top of the water, flat and bare and empty, with no life upon it."

Ishi died in 1916 in San Francisco.

*Theodora Kroeber, *Ishi: Last of His Tribe* (Berkeley: Parnassus Press, 1964), 27.

The Yellow Primrose

WINTER'S ON ITS DOWNHILL RUN, spring is possible, and the shops are selling little pots of primroses. Primroses, *prima rosa*, red, pink, purple, white, vermilion, magenta—and *yellow*, the perfect yellow of the wild primrose.

Primroses stop me in my tracks when I see them in the shops. I love their rich colors, the very colors of spring. But it's the yellow blossoms that move me most. Hardly anything designates *trout* to me more persuasively or more appealingly than a yellow primrose.

Once upon a lovely late spring day in Ireland, Ned Cusack was walking me up and over a hill near Kells to drop down onto a remote stretch of the Kells Blackwater that he loved. The yellow primrose was in such array that we could not avoid stepping on them. In memory they have become the emblem of a wonderful day with the colonel and those brown trout—all trout, in fact.

And then, back on these shores, when one falls under the spell of that great old Pennsylvanian angler and wet-fly tyer, Jim Leisenring, one must also fall under the spell of what must have been his favorite color: *primrose yellow*. Pearsall's Gossamer tying silk and Corticelli's Button Hole Twist, both in primrose yellow, were his indispensables. A bit of dun mole fur spun onto

39

primrose yellow tying silk might just be, along with peacock herl, the most essential body of a trout fly. Just let the primrose yellow of the silk show through the dub, and when wet, the effect will be perfect both for trout and angler.

Writing the words *primrose yellow* over and over here does it for me—primes me for the coming of spring and a new season, a season in which everything will be lovely and fresh and full of life. Of course it won't be that way at all, we know that, but the primrose blooming in field or shop suggests that it might be so. . . .

In the meantime, I'll keep a spool of Pearsall's Gossamer thread and Corticelli's Button Hole Twist in primrose yellow silk close at hand to turn my thoughts to Big Jim Leisenring, Ned Cusack, the Blackwater trout—and the anticipation of nature's renewal.

MUCH ADO
OR WHAT SHAKESPEARE KNEW

> *The pleasant'st angling is to see the fish*
> *Cut with her golden oars the silver stream*
> *And greedily devour the treacherous bait.*
> —*Much Ado about Nothing,* Act III, scene 1

The Silver Salver

WALK INTO ONE OF THOSE INVITING SMALL FISHING HOTELS in Ireland or Scotland, or in England for that matter, and it's likely that just inside the front door, on your left, there will be a small table on which rests a large silver salver with handles to it. On your right, again most likely, will be the door into the dining room. Dead ahead, the stairs will rise to your room above, and somewhere down the hall from where you stand will be a cozy little bar upon which the felicity of this experience so much depends. And it's from those depths down the hallway that the manager of the hotel will come to welcome you.

But let me pull your attention back to that big silver tray on the table just inside the door. If you are arriving late in the afternoon or early evening, or if, already in residence, you are coming down for dinner, there may be lying on that tray the salmon—singular or plural—that were taken from the hotel's water that day. The magnificent fish, even if only a grilse, are especially beautiful, displayed rampant on that tray. Alongside each fish is a discreet card giving the fish's weight, the fly that took it, the beat where it took, and the resident of the hotel who took it. It is proof positive of a resident angler's success—or failure—and there's no nonsense about it because, by long and gentle tradition, residents always give their fish up for this daily exhibition for all the guests in the hotel to see as they proceed in to dinner—a dinner not unlikely featuring one of the salmon caught and displayed here just yesterday.

Surely this is one of the most delightful of the many minor rituals surrounding the highly ritualistic pursuit of the Atlantic salmon.

The dining rooms of most ordinary small hotels where guests put up for more than a night or two are usually astir with undercurrents of comment and speculation about who's wearing what awful suit or dress, about position in society, if any, about who's worth how much and how they came by it—or worse, adulteries far and wide, who's unfaithful to whom, and is it going on right now in this very hotel, etc., etc. It's a great game, but it can be quite painful to one who is neither a regular at the hotel nor secure in the manner born.

In a *fishing* hotel, on the other hand, with those fish out there in the hall on that silver salver, all this ordinary sort of gossip fades into mere white noise in the background, while the really lively talk is all about who caught what, how, where, when, and why didn't I do as well. . . . It may even be about whom the management may be favoring with the most productive beats on the river.

There develops a ranking of the guests, at the top of which is the one who puts more fish day by day on that tray out there in the hall. He becomes lord of the dining room. All of this is highly subtle and decorous, but there it is: a hierarchy of guests depending on who can most frequently plop a fish—or the biggest—down on the silver salver.

Of course, the more fish on the tray, the better for the management. Every fish denotes a satisfied guest who may be expected to return again next season. And in many of these hotels, the management retains a part interest in each fish caught.

But it's the guest whose luck has not been good who so desperately wants to put a fish on that table—to join the party as it were, to be able to enter into the hotel gossip somewhere up off the bottom of the pecking order—not from the position of an always defeated fisherman.

But you are not to fret overly much as you come back to the hotel after a day on the river, passing by that table and salver without a salmon of your own. All's not competition, envy, and gossip. More often than not, there's an evening of good feeling, relaxed cordiality, quick new friendships of the moment, and excellent fishing talk in both bar and dining room. The most successful anglers are frequently eager to stand drinks all round—and so the bar hums. On those really good days, rare enough, when everyone takes a fish, the pleasure of the bar, of the dining room, and of the evening in good company can be memorable.

RITUAL AND THE FLY

Ritual: a representative action, often a custom,
potent with meaning drawn from habit,
memory, belief, or tradition; observed
in common or in private.

As human culture has moved through time and, generally speaking, from east to west, it has tended to move from a density of ritual practice to the more empirical and analytical.

We like to think that as moderns we have "demystified" our belief systems and so have reduced the need and use of ritual in representing those systems.

As angling moved from east to west, from its origins, as we moderns know it, in the British Isles and Ireland, it moved from an elegant, precisely ritualized practice to a more inventive, open, improvisational spirit and approach. The rituals of British angling strongly influenced early eastern American ways. But as trout fishing moved into western America, ritual trappings tended to fall away.

Vincent Marinaro held that "fly fishing" up until the mid-twentieth century had meant essentially "mayfly fishing," fishing to that insect, the ephemeral life of which is so highly ritualized. But with the speed-up of the westward movement, the trout fly has been increasingly demystified and deritualized and so has tended to become less and less a mayfly and more an "attractor fly" intended to attract just about any fish that swims.

We feel that we have become quite clearheaded, sensible, and analytical about most everything, rather smug, in fact, even about our fishing and its equipment, to say nothing of our behavior on and off the stream—no silver salvers for us, please.

But empiricism, analysis, and improvisation can dry up on us and leave us longing for the lost riches and assurances of ritual. And to satisfy that longing, aren't there now signs and portents of new angling rituals struggling to surface? Isn't catch and release itself a ritual, not a very pretty one, but a ritual nonetheless? Isn't ritual at the core of human experience—and the spirit's anchor? And aren't we always reinventing it? Today's analysis becomes tomorrow's mystery, enhanced by its own battery of ritual—just as East becomes West and West in turn becomes a new East.

In a New Jersey Garden
Forsythian Parabolas

WHEN I VISITED HERE A COUPLE OF EASTERS AGO, the forsythia in this New Jersey garden were in full, rampant bloom. They reminded me that old-timers over in Pennsylvania held that when the forsythia bloomed, the Hendrickson—*Ephemerella subvaria*—came off. The long, graceful boughs of golden bloom, waving gently, also suggested the graceful motion of the cast of a fly, perhaps a Hendrickson, over easy flowing waters.

That experience found its way into the verses of "In a New Jersey Garden," which appeared in my *Notes from an Old Fly Book.*

Today, two years later and nearer to midsummer, in this same garden, the masses of yellow flowers are gone, the boughs now burdened with new green foliage, upturning. The bend, the curve, of each bough is clear to see and resembles a parabola.

That elegant curve recalls for me today our enthusiasm, right after World War II, for "parabolic fly rods," rods whose bend, or "action," also suggested a parabola. In these new rods, the action or flex began deep in the butt section, under the hand, and progressed upward to gather energy and power in the midsection before handing the work of the cast over to the substantial tip. Just like a limb of forsythia.

*Forsythian parabolic in a New Jersey garden, 2002,
drawing by John Betts.*

They were powerful rods, slow, strong, and hard to damage. If they inclined to the heavy side, they were, in the right hands, superb distance casters. Their enemies called them sluggish, soft, and indelicate—or worse, like the spineless, old-time "wet fly" action rods.

Needless to say, these new rods of half a century ago were of cane—before the introduction of fiberglass and a long generation away from the hard-bitten carbon "attack" rods of today.

Immediately after the war, a renaissance of cane rod building got under way based on wartime waterproof marine glues that were stronger even than bamboo fiber itself. In New York, Louis B. Feierabend had just invented and was manufacturing the brilliant Super Z ferrule and so solved forever one of the most vexing of all bamboo rod construction problems.

With the new glues and the new ferrules, American Tonkin cane rods were the finest fishing rods in the world. (Few fly fishermen today have lived through cane, glass, and carbon and realize that cane is the most indestructible of the three rod materials.)

Parabolics were the new sensation.

The illustrious Charles Ritz, great Parisian hotelier and passionate fly fisher, was perhaps the first to advocate and manufacture parabolic fly rods. A. J. McClane wrote several probing and surprisingly technical columns about this new rod design in *Field and Stream* and professed to admire them. One of the greatest of all American rod builders, Paul Young of Detroit, took up their manufacture and made a significant number of discerning anglers devotees of the new bend.

Still, the average fly caster never quite liked the true parabolic. It was not quite as *forgiving* a rod as it had been touted to be. It was too soft, too slow, and required careful timing in order to prevent the cast's falling back on itself. In the hands of many, the rods felt tip heavy, as though the tip were being *dragged* along through the cast instead of contributing dynamically to it. It was just too specialized a rod action ever to become popular.

But the idea wouldn't go away. Rods with "modified parabolic action" appeared, with more stuff in the butt and lighter, more sensitive tips. Some called them "progressive action." One could still sense a nice progression smoothly up the rod to a responsive tip joint. (Almost all the fine new cane rods were made in two pieces, three pieces being thought quite old-fashioned.) Lou Feierabend, of great ferrule fame, while developing machinery and rod tapers for Nat Uslan's five-strip construction, thought from the beginning that anglers would not accept a rod that bent under the hand and argued with Ulsan for a swelled butt on his progressive tapers. He wanted a rod that would sturdy up the cast and throw more and quicker energy into the tip section.

Ah! But not like those prewar, weak-tipped "dry fly actions" of old, which simply could not stand up under the strain of modern power-stroke casting. It's important to recognize that this modern American fly casting after World War II came under the influence, if not the control, of the West Coast, San Francisco anglers who wanted to throw big flies a hundred feet over big water to rampaging steelhead. They needed rods that would stand up under incessant double hauling, not to mention heavy fish. This "modified parabolic" (the word *parabolic* rather quickly dropped from the angling lexicon) or "progressive action" did superbly well.

Winston and Powell made these rods in the far West, Bill Phillipson tried them in Denver, Paul Young mastered them in Detroit, and Nat Uslan and Lou Feierabend built them out of five strips in New York. Fly rods were never to be the same again. Everywhere the new American Masters dominated the field, making the finest rods that the world had ever seen—before or since.

And so fishing goes on and on, inexorably connecting everything to everything else—or seeming to. A garden full of forsythia has much to tell us about our fishing.

What's More...

It's a crying shame that a fine fly rod must be known and named by the size of something else, like the size of a line. I flinch when I hear an angler say, "I took him on my three weight."

In the first place, I think that designated line sizes for rods are not nearly as specific and binding as manufacturers say and we accept. On a given day, any good rod can throw three lines, depending on the caster and the intention of the cast. Furthermore, no line-size designation can describe the bend or character of a rod, where it lies between slow and fast, full flex and tip accentuated.

When cane was the nearly exclusive rod material, anglers tended to identify their rods by maker and length: "I took him on my eight-foot Granger," for instance. If another dimension of description were needed, they might give rod weight, their "three-and-a-half-ounce Granger." Of course, good rod makers almost always inked onto the cane just above the grip a recommended line size: *HDH* or *HCH,* for instance—lines based on the weight of silk. These terms didn't tell us everything about a rod, but they were not expected to.

When we were really serious about our rods and wanted to say more about them in order to describe their casting character, we gave rod length and the diameters of ferrule and tip top in 64ths of an inch. An eight footer on a ^{14}/64ths ferrule and a ^{6}/64ths tip top would tend to lie in the "parabolic" range described in the essay above. Take ^{1}/64th off that tip dimension and the rod became "modified" or "progressive." In this way we knew how much cane was in a rod and roughly how it was distributed. We knew where we were at—a whole lot more than by mentioning only a sort of ballpark line weight. A good rod deserves better talk from us.

His Brain

THIS FRIEND OF MINE SAYS THAT EVERY SINGLE DAY, as he gets older and older, he enjoys his brain more and more. A striking, wonderful thing to say, it seems to me.

Come to think of it, this brain of ours is the most powerful and versatile device in all the universe—at least as far as we know. It has this astonishing ability not only to accomplish its amazing feats, but to *observe* itself doing them and, what's more, to *enjoy* the act of observation!

The brain's at once the most singular thing in all creation and as common as dirt. Every mother's daughter and son has one for his or her very own, even to take out fishing in order to sit atop our neuromuscular system and accomplish wonders.

Let's think for a moment of fly rods. Let's imagine that we need to cast a fly forty-five feet up into a slot of water two feet wide. Let's mark it out on the lawn and try it. We'll have four different fly rods of eight feet but of different weights, tapers, and casting characteristics. I submit that we will take up each rod in its turn, wave it in the air a couple of times, and then make the required cast more or less satisfactorily.

The moral of the story is that it's not so much the design of the rod that makes the *big* difference, but the caster's experienced, seemingly miraculous neuromuscular system that reads the problem and the rod, each one of those flexible eight-foot sticks, and almost immediately knows how to do the work at hand. How otherwise would so many different anglers, using quite different rods, cast successfully to that fish rising forty-five feet upstream in that narrow slot of bright water?

Give us a long flexible stick and a line of adequate weight and we can do it. And just think, we *all* have the means to do it, that gift of a brain, with which to do this wonderful thing and—free of charge!

FROM SUCH STUFF

In Spain I wanted the bus to stop
To let me out to touch a cork oak tree
And think of gripping my good old rods.

I wished the bus might roll right on to Murcia
Where I could see a silkworm spinning
Silk for winding those venerable sticks.

Maybe I could find a fiery forge
Drawing wire—chrome steel and tough
To guide a line on them.

I always watch for German nickel silver
Lustrous soft and warm
To join a rod and hold a reel.

But it was in that ancient Kyoto garden
In its sacred precincts
That I dared to leave the path

And enter a bamboo stand
Of giant silent culms.
Standing close I felt their living skins
And put my ear to one—
With my knuckles knocked on it
And heard the treasure of the cane in my old rods.
↜ GMW

A Fly Line Tangled

IN THE OLD DAYS, WHEN A BOY OF THIRTEEN CAME DOWN SICK, his mother, likely as not, put him to bed for the day. And so with me on an early spring day when, though my belly ached, I could think of little but the coming fishing season.

On the Christmas just past, my parents had given me a nicely refinished old cane fly rod, a South Bend Orenomatic fly reel, and a Weber Henshall silk fly line: level, size E. Just about my most wonderful Christmas present ever.

Somehow I got that new, beautifully coiled line into my sickbed with me. The oiled silk was fragrant and supple, filling the room with fantasies of the season to come. I couldn't leave it alone and soon loosed the coil and had it all over the bed in a hopeless tangle. I could do nothing with it. I had fouled up, or so it seemed, not just the line, but my whole world, which the line came to represent just then.

I remember, in my panic, calling to my mother for help. In she came, sat quietly on the bed, and carefully untangled the line—and restored its perfect coil.

Then, with never a hint of fault for me, in her lovely and generous way, she went about her work, little realizing that she had untangled more than just that Weber fly line: she had straightened out the mess that I was sure I had just made of my whole young life.

Over the years, I've wondered at the way people like my mother make these casually loving gestures or say those unforgettable words of kindness that rescue us from the desperate tangles of frightening experience and get us back into order and love.

JIMMY CARTER

I'll venture that Jimmy Carter is the finest and most effective ex-president we've had since Thomas Jefferson. And now a Nobel laureate.

Jimmy Carter is a devoted fly fisherman, but I don't suggest that fishing has had anything to do with making him what he is. I do take heart, however, in the thought that there is something or other in fly fishing that can appeal to a man like Carter.

The Rise of the Crafts
How We Got This Great New Tackle!

AFTER THE MASTERS OF THE PREWAR TWENTIETH CENTURY had accomplished their groundbreaking work in fine fishing tackle, why, in the last quarter of that century, should there have burgeoned such a remarkable and vast development in the practical arts and crafts of fishing, especially fly fishing? What were the conditions that led to reconceiving and making the new and superb cane rods,* exquisite reels, flies defying description—every ingenious accouterment we anglers could desire?

I suggest that this phenomenon had it origins in the Kennedy enthusiasms of the early sixties and got up steam in the ensuing turbulence of radical protest, when young people, caught up in the Movement, believed that a craft object from their own hand was a visible and outward sign of inner grace.† Their craft-arts: their pots and jewelry, their clothing, music, and writing, while intended to be both useful and attractive were more importantly the show of an inward beauty that was proof positive of the righteousness of radical causes espoused. At least that was the *faith implicit*—and *The Whole Earth Catalog* was its gospel.

In the early 1950s, as the nation was recovering from World War II, the guiding ethos, the trope, under which objects for recreation and decorative enjoyment were crafted was that of *industry*.

A decade later, concurrent with the impact and force of John Kennedy in the White House, social conditions changed rapidly. The guiding ethos, the trope, of that new force, and the *new craftsmanship* that helped to express it, was something akin to a *new freedom*—or, perhaps, that word carved into a stone mandala in Central Park, across from The Dakota: *Imagine*.

The handmade craft object, complete from its single maker, was a projection of the maker's spirit, defined by an affinity with nature, peacefulness, generosity, anti-materialism, and anti-authority, with commitment to all oppressed peoples—all the values cried, sometimes hysterically, by the revolutionary young of those days. That their crafts were as often as not trite and amateurish in no way affects the argument.

Crafts could be an act of defiance against the Establishment, which, in its turn, jealously guarded the *high* arts as its own special province. Crafts, on the other hand, were and are essentially democratic and often tinged with revolutionary feeling. Anybody can do it—make a craft object—the poor as well as the rich. Democracy thrives in the crafts.

But it's more complicated than that. Crafts have commonly memorialized an ideal of the past. We can see this pattern working in England in the nineteenth century. Craftsmanship, as a way of life, burgeoned suddenly among English intellectuals, artists, and artisans under the leadership of William Morris. The movement was in commemoration of what Morris and his radical followers felt were the glories of the Middle Ages, when craftsmen were also supreme artists. Those years saw dedicated and anonymous medieval craftsmen building and decorating the Gothic churches. They saw monks illuminating manuscripts and crafting liturgical drama and music, women—*secular* and *regular*—weaving brilliant tapestries and church raiments. These arts, crafts, and their guilds were thought, by their rediscoverers, to be high human achievement and profoundly humane. In the spirit of thinkers like William Morris, the program was anti-industrial, anti-urban, anti-capitalist, and deeply spiritual.

As in Morris's life and work, the crafts have usually been associated with socialist ideals and visions of a genuine democratic future. While Morris took for inspiration what he perceived as the humanity of the Middle Ages, the rougher activist Luddites in England played their part by threatening to destroy the machines that threatened their handwork livelihoods. Handcraftsmanship became and has remained open to ideology—the protest, sometimes profoundly subtle, of outsiders in defiance of masters.

Little wonder that the sixties children in their communes took to making stuff, trying to invest it with their spirit in order to prove the justice of their causes. They projected craftsmanship out into the cultural air of their times, where their work and imagination became a cultural *force* that remains with us today—not only among leftover hippies, but all who, influenced by them, caught that new cultural air. Not only were they dedicated: some had genuine artistic ability, some real technical insight, and together they wrought fine and useful things.

Though numbers of the kids had disposable cash from parental support and trusts, their domestic economy was a nagging problem: how to live on the meager remunerations of their craftsmanship? Others, who took up the king's shilling of a more regular life and "went straight"—or were co-opted—may still look back with a sense of having been on the scene of big events and ideas in those important days.

The causes that united the kids of the sixties into communities have now dwindled into a generic, undirected, anti-establishment, anti-social funkiness. The cooperative spirit of that seminal decade has converted into a harsh neo-individualism that retreats from public and social values. It's a tone felt in many of the shops and studios, here and there, where craftsmen do their solitary work.

It's fair to wonder how long these artisans can keep it up. Makers of tackle even now must cope with the ruthless pressures of the conventional marketplace, where the manufacture of fishing tackle is now referred to as *The Industry* and fisheries as *The Resource*. This sort of thinking, in a slack economy, may well be the ruin of the idealism of those still trying to work in the splendid and spirited isolation of craftsmanship.

But then, earlier, classical communal efforts didn't work either. The famous cooperatives of the nineteenth century failed in the face of economic necessity, cultural vulgarity, and social decay, to say nothing of their own naiveté.

Still, the crafts, making handsome, useful objects, are one of the last outposts against the depredations of cybernetic, *virtual* life and its banal uniformity. They are one of the most important and available means of personal expression, the expression that Emerson insisted all people so sorely need.

So for now, a few old hippies and the many in their cultural tradition, some still opposing this or that, are at their work benches making things. Combining tradition with inspiration, they now make the finest fly rods and reels anglers have ever known. They tie incomparable flies, regularly bringing forth the new and the elegant. They invent every sort of accessory in cottage-scaled industries, where handwork still rules the working day—right here in the United States.

They take us back in the imagination to a better time before the captains of corporations taught us to behave ourselves, know our place, and properly appreciate the rewards of post-Reagan consumerism.

There may never have been a time quite that ideal, but its possibility can be memorialized in a fine cane fly rod that remains an act of subtle defiance of crass consumerism—an act so hard for politicians to understand, those who feel obligated to denounce the legacy of the sixties in order to prove their conservative credentials. They see that legacy as a threat to their idea of society and so refuse to recognize that the free-ranging human spirit, as in those turbulent sixties, is always there, just around the corner of events, waiting to be called forth to change things and perhaps once again leave behind imaginative new objects as its sign.

*We must remember that World War II stimulated much new development in all our gear. For instance, the new marine glues made the renaissance of cane rod design and building in the late 1940s a practical matter.

†What happened in the art of the theatre during this same period is nicely analogous to this matter of the crafts. The one is much like and sheds light on the other. It was in that common spirit that in 1972 I began teaching a new college course that I called "The Post-Modern Theatre."

THE CARIBOU CAPTAIN

I feel constrained to reveal my one secret and indispensable fly, the dry Caribou Captain, so called for its color resemblance to the old western wet fly The Captain and for its wing of caribou hair. Here it is. It's a good one, and, I believe, covers a multitude of evils on the stream.

    hook size: 16 and 18
    tail: none
    body: thin, finely dubbed black
    hackle: palmered Whiting dyed brown grizzly saddle
    wing: light gray caribou hair
    head: stubs of wing hair à la Elk Hair Caddis

Tie in a length of fine copper wire at bend and then dub the body. Tie in hackle and take two or maybe three turns at thorax before palmering back to the bend, there to secure it with four turns of the copper wire. Tie in caribou hair wing, which should stand upright and flare. Leave a head of hair stubs. The correct caribou hair is hard to find. A good bright gray deer hair works well enough. Finally, trim off hackle close to body underneath the hook in a wide V to make it sit down close on the surface.

Remembering Trout Fishing in America
aka Richard Brautigan, 1935–1984

YOU MAY SAY TO YOURSELF WHEN YOU READ THIS, "How strange!" Even, "How absurd." But listen for a moment: indulge me. Back in those turbulent sixties, which, if you are fifty or over, must resonate to some extent within you, there appeared, in 1967, a little book called *Trout Fishing in America,* by Richard Brautigan, one of that San Francisco counterculture gang of writers.

Brautigan accomplished the literary feat of finding a frame of reference for the horrors of warfare and the social-economic evils of his time in *trout fishing.* Trout fishing: the idea of it became Brautigan's *way out,* a way to save himself, a way of answering a bad world with a novel!

But what a strange sort-of novel it is, not unlike an extended poem, the shattered dream of a madman, a "spaced-out" biography, an almost religious appeal to the saving grace of trout fishing in those terrible times. A masterwork in any case. No one had written a novel like that before, nor, I think, since. I vividly recall picking up my copy at the City Lights Book Store in San Francisco in '67 or '68 and being swept up into I then knew not what.

I used to tell my students that fishing was the only sport that had contributed a masterpiece, Izaak Walton's *The Compleat Angler,* to world literature. I think now that fishing has contributed a similar masterpiece to American literature, to say nothing of angling literature, in *Trout Fishing in America.* I say this in the teeth of the too often automatic response to Brautigan's book, that it's not really about trout fishing. Wrong!

In the middle of the night not long ago, I couldn't keep the book from banging around in my head and had to get up and come down to this machine to pound out a slew of words about this wild and brilliant book. It struck me then that Brautigan's book is not unlike Walton's. Both arose from a similar psychological need and sociological criticism. Both writers solved their dire problems in the comforts and crazinesses of fishing! I felt Walton and Brautigan reaching together across the centuries— and that it was angling that brought them together in their similar views of the world and experience.

And so for days and days I worked on those words, relentlessly cutting them down to what you see here below and discovering a form for them—a sort of *confession of faith* as a tribute to Brautigan and his wonderful book. It's faith in both *him* and in Walton, in fishing, and in the justice of the causes that so painfully and memorably drove both men to go fishing and to write about it. Now to those words with which I hope at last to lodge Brautigan permanently in angling literature:

The Confession of *Trout Fishing in America*

O Brautigan, O Excellent Richard Brautigan,
Trout Fishing in America,
Forgive us in this hour of our need.
We've forgotten you and your little book.*
1967!
Think of It!
O Richard Brautigan,
from those thrilling days of yesteryear,
when California schooless schools of scribblers,
writing better through chemistry,
sought to free their writing from *meanings*
that were good for nothing but wasting a life,
making war and rumors of war
and a deep death inside.
When suddenly The Heavens opened and you, Richard,
In the Paradise of your Mind, became
Trout Fishing in America!
And went fishing in a Wilderness of Freedom,
wading and casting that purest river of the mind—
that secondhand trout stream
purchased from the **Cleveland Wrecking Yard** out there in
San Francisco, where regular lengths of old trout stream,
stacked like timbers, sold for
$6.50 the running foot.

But you left us stuck in a Wretched Third Millennium of
Issues, Programs, and Projects
of denatured, TU, TV fishing
in rivers of dreary writing running through it—
fishing for recycled, graphite-whipped trout
that we try to believe are the real thing.

How innocent seem those Brautigan sixties now!
Just a few feet of used trout stream from which to catch
Flashes of Life!

O Richard Brautigan, pray for us.
***Trout Fishing in America,* pray for us.**
Maria Callas, pray for us
(while as sweethearts you eat your golden apples).

Mozart, O Mozart!
Have mercy upon us!

*New York: Dell, 1967.

TFIA Notes

An Emergency Kit of Annotations for The Confession of
Trout Fishing in America

Kit Model No. BrautTFIA67/02.1

To be read only in case of emergency

Confession, as in "confession of faith," at a particular place and time.

little book = *Trout Fishing in America.*

thrilling days of yesteryear, as in Lone Ranger broadcasts... better through chemistry, as in DuPont logo.

TU = Trout Unlimited, a national advocacy organization for salmonid protection. Better than nothing, but boring.

rivers . . . running through it, as in the title of popular but now boring novella and film.

graphite, as in the synthetic carbon material out of which fishing rods are currently being made—also boring.

Maria Callas, arguably the greatest soprano of the twentieth century. Never, never boring.

golden apples, what apples?

Mozart, Mozart always has the last word about everything, coming and going, then and now, and hereinafter.

Richard Brautigan killed himself in 1984 at the age of forty-nine.

RICHARD BRAUTIGAN: A BIOGRAPHICAL NOTE
AKA
Trout Fishing in America

Richard Gary Brautigan, poet and novelist. Born: Tacoma, Washington, January 30, 1935. Died by his own hand, 1984. Called "the Last of the Beats." A cult figure of the 1960s.

At twenty, after throwing a stone through a police station window in order to go to jail and get something to eat, Brautigan was sent to the Oregon State Hospital instead where he was diagnosed as schizophrenic and given electric shock therapy.

Upon release, he migrated south to San Francisco and became a popular figure in the hippie movement. Tall and gangly, with long blond hair, a bent back, and granny glasses, he epitomized the hippie.

During the summer of 1961, while camping out along Idaho trout streams with his wife and daughter, he drafted what would become his finest work, *Trout Fishing in America*.

Brautigan committed suicide in 1984, two years after the publication of his last novel.

On Don Quixote, Adventure, and Getting Wet for Trout

DEAR READER, WE KNOW HOW THE BELOVED AND DEMENTED Don Quixote de la Mancha, the Knight of the Sad Countenance, in his effort to revive knight errantry set out with his faithful squire, Sancho Panza, on his Adventures through Spain to rescue fair maidens and succor widows and the downtrodden, and how the immortal knight and his squire first came upon a line of windmills that became, in Don Quixote's crazed imagination, horrible and cruel Giants. Without hesitation, Don Quixote lowered his lance and rode his emaciated dear old Rocinante against them—to the first of his terrible tumbles.

Miguel Cervantes's sixteenth-century history of that most famous of knights-errant was to become the world's first and probably greatest novel, comic or otherwise. He and Shakespeare died on the same day in 1616.

But what many of us, even anglers, are unlikely to know is that a delightful, 1998 collection of adages about fishing from one of our finest angling authors tells us that somewhere in the thousand pages of record of Don Quixote and Sancho's adventuring lies the pithy proverb or maxim:

There is no taking trout in dry breeches.

On the twenty-fifth of September, 1996, I sat in extraordinary comfort in the guest-house cloisters of the Franciscan Monastery of Guadalupe in Extremadura, Spain, and finished my first reading of Don Quixote. And, with the driest sherry and excellent local olives, I held my breath in wonder of the experience of this great book. I thanked my lucky stars that I had waited until I was past seventy to read it, when I was fully prepared (which is to say, had become an old fool myself) for it—and in the remote mountains of Spain to boot.

But, I hasten to add, nowhere in the text had I noted that Cervantes, the Don, or Sancho Panza had remarked that trout fishing means getting one's pants wet. I had not seen it. Is it conceivable that I had missed it? Me!

Having missed—apparently—seeing this wonderful proverb, which sounds like Sancho Panza, the first time through the book, I recently dedicated myself to an Adventure of my own to discover and capture the elusive proverb. And so I embarked on a second reading, entering the novel and snooping along the trail of the knightly, mad Don Quixote.

Many of you who are devoted to Cervantes and Don Quixote will remember that there is probably no work of fiction in which so many aphorisms, proverbs, and wise old sayings are so densely packed. Sancho Panza is worst of all. Often it takes him a dozen or more aphorisms strung together in order to make one of those pithy points about life for which we so love and treasure him. The one about wet breeches could be anywhere in those thousand pages. I was in for a close reading.

I scoured the text line by line, day after day, but found it nowhere. And now here I am with only a few pages left to read that will take me to Don Quixote's deathbed in his home village. Could the proverb still lie ahead in these few remaining pages? My Adventure draws to a close. I feel that I have been following with a full heart close behind the Don on his Rocinante and Sancho on Dapple, the donkey that he loves better than life itself. I'm close behind as they ride closer and closer to home, toward the restoration of the Don's sanity, his forswearing knight-errantry, and his peaceful death in his serene old age in his own bed.

But the great sadness is that he never once was to catch a glimpse of that sublime, most beautiful lady to whom as knight-errant he was devoted and who was the inspiration of his knightly quests: the perfection of all womanhood, Dulcinea del Toboso. Never in the entire history of Don Quixote was she to be seen. Why?

Why? Because she was a creature of the Don's madness. The only way he could explain his inability to find her throughout his many Adventures was that he felt himself always beset by an Axis of Evil Enchanters, supernatural enemies, who were bound to frustrate his nearly every effort at chivalric love and heroism. These Enchanters, he felt sure, had gone so far as to transform the divine Dulcinea into an ugly, pug-nosed peasant girl in order to prevent his fulfilling his life's greatest dream—the presentation of himself to Dulcinea and receiving from her his charge of Knighthood, Love, and Adventure. No wonder he could not find her—she who can exist only in the imagination. Without her, in the fullness of her person, Don Quixote is left (as aren't we all?) on feet of clay, flawed, painfully given even to his random rages, violence, and meanness of spirit.

My quest for the saying *There is no taking trout in dry breeches* is perhaps a day's ride behind Don Quixote—in the last pages of my second reading of the novel in a decade—and still I cannot find it. I am given to believe that I too am enchanted, that a Black-Hearted Gang of Duplicitous Enchanters of a Third Millennium Variety are out to get me. They will not let me see those words, as line by line I have searched for them. They impugn my sometime credit as critic of literature, angler, and human being. Could it be that they are hiding the missing maxim in order to cheat me of my search—as so often happened to the great Don himself?

My aim had been innocent enough. I merely wanted to recount how, over all the ages, anglers have aspired to stay dry when out there fishing—when, long ago, those who went before us on the water had no proper gear for staying dry at all. I wanted to show that even in *our* time, and not so long ago at that, it was hard enough to keep our breeches dry even in the finest available wading gear. But now, in this late age of miraculous synthetic fibers, we can stay dry and "breathable" most all of the time and so can afford a generous nod of fellowship to those anglers of old, of Cervantes's sixteenth century and his immortal Don Quixote—a hero no more mad in his pursuit of knight-errantry than we in our crazy chasing after the trout. We remember, all too well, playing the fool ourselves and getting soaked and half frozen for our pains.

Finally, now that I have apparently failed in my Adventure, failed to find that wonderful proverb for you, my angling friends, I suspect that I have failed because of the enchantment in which I am held by those bastards out there who intend no good to me. I shall always suspect that there are those whose business it is to prevent my finding saving passages in great books, good fishing, and any reason at all to explain the madness of the world that broke the heart of the noble Don Quixote and is ruining ours. I am prevented because those Enchanters don't want me to find any such abiding and loaded-with-truth proverb about fishing. Next thing, I'd presume to look for Dulcinea herself!

The Enchanters, interested only in their power to destroy, don't want anybody ever to discover the divine Dulcinea del Toboso and the liberation that attends on her.

And so we give up and go home. With the great Don Quixote, I, in my small way, have lost the innocence and the idealism of a lovely madness and must now be content. Or should I...?

Wait! Stop! I've found it!
Or have I?
Good grief! It's only *half* of it!
Eighteen pages from the end of part II,
On page 922 of the J. M. Cohen Penguin edition,
In chapter 71,
In the Last Days of Don Quixote's Life,
At 5:00 PM on this Sunday, the first day of June 2003,
here it is:
Sancho says,
...for you don't catch trout...I say no more.

But where's the second half about getting wet?
Did Cervantes omit it?
This morning I learned that the full proverb in
the original Spanish reads:

No se toman truchas
A bragas enjutas.

Two Hours Later!

I have just learned from a professor at the University of Colorado that, indeed, Cervantes did give *only the first half of the maxim,* that it is so well known that he could count on his every Spanish reader to complete it for himself. The professor tells me that in the fullest version of the maxim—that most everyone would know—there occurs the naughty word *culo,* or "ass." As in, "*You don't catch trout without getting your ass wet!*" Sancho is reluctant to utter the "bad" word and so dodges it with, "*I say no more.*"

Though the Enchanters have been at work to frustrate me at every point and leave me Up the Creek..., I am gradually escaping. One Enchanter-Translator, Burton Raffel, is so pernicious as to render our proverb:

"...you won't get what you want...but I won't say any more."
The Devil in him then tells us that the full proverb—denatured by his cutting out the allusion to fishing for trout—means:
"You won't get what you want if you just sit on your ass."
Indeed!
A fine way to treat a noble sentiment about angling!
So now...
My quest is done. I have achieved what I could for
the idea of angling in Don Quixote

The Duds We Wear

Just think for a moment about the way we appear out on the stream—how we're dressed. I say nothing about those who go out all bright and garish or, worse, half undressed, but of us who care about the image we cut on the water. To see ourselves as others see us, look at fly-fishing videos, catalogs, the shops, as well as other anglers in the field.

Overall we look pretty good, what with those fine postmodern, postneoprene waders—"breathables" in the classic cut and color—with our ensembles bottomed out with good-looking, well-designed wading shoes and topped off with Lee Wulff–type vests and a dashing hat. Add on all those other stylish vanities of the stream of which the shops are full.

So why pay any attention? I guess it's because we all tend to look alike, almost in uniform. At a distance we often can't be distinguished one from the other. And sad to say, that uniform has become international! We've been standardized.

Once upon a time, anglers looked quite different from each other. When I was growing up, ordinary fishermen wore their rough work clothes or cast-off street dress on the stream. If those years were paradoxically the golden age of fly fishing, as some maintain, anglers who could afford it regarded their sartorial image with care. They required a variety of custom, conservative sporting clothes from which to choose a wardrobe. How different from the sameness of the current mass-produced, regularized, and hyper-marketed fly-fishing gear that we wear today! Just look at the old photographs!

Back then an angler had to invent himself and his image, as it were, out of whole cloth and live by it. The results were often striking. *Kleider machen Leute* is the German aphorism: "Clothes make the man!" I was raised to believe that dressing well was next almost to godliness, and now here I am with my old man's gut compromising the way I look and causing my wife to remark that I don't look quite up to snuff anymore when fishing. Maybe I'm too careless or just can't cut a neat unified, compact figure out there anymore.... Maybe my old front and back pouched Letort-type tackle pack isn't as snappy as the conventional vest.... I don't know. I'd like to look better—but not just like everybody else.

Maybe by paying close-up attention to our shirtfronts, collars, and neckwear, we could claim attention as individuals, each in his own right. My father told me that the essential thing in a man's dress was to get the necktie and collar right, even impeccable. Maybe that would work for the fisherman as well....

A couple of years ago, I saw two gorgeous young women fishing Long Lake, both elegantly and glamorously turned out, with just the right equipment. They turned my head nearly off my shoulders.

It's important, whatever we wear, not to look *brand-spanking new*, just out of the shop. We need to look experienced, well run-in, even worn. (You can't beat bloodstains on your waders.) We ought to avoid being overaccessorized or at least keep the fussy gadgets hidden away in the secret recesses of the vest.

Anyway, I wish I knew what to wear without looking "in uniform." Years ago, Wshing the Coln in England's Cotswolds, I wore a proper three-piece herringbone tweed suit, a nice tie, and a smart hat.

I might just say, "To hell with it," and do that again over here!

Angling and the Class Struggle

THE CLASS STRUGGLE IN FISHING! CAN IT BE? WELL, YES! People on opposite sides of the social-economic tracks have forever been locked in struggle of one kind or another. Always a serious business.

From the end of the Civil War until World War II, a bona fide *upper class* held sway even in a supposedly classless America. It was their *gilded age,* in which fishing was part of the polish.

American anglers back then were fishing almost within living memory of the edenic New World continent to which their forbears had come and where they would develop a New World way of life, including sport with abundant fishing for everyone, rich and poor. The lingering dream of the pastoral life in which all people might live together in amity and abundance, regardless of their positions and fortunes, still had force. But not enough: the world was going modern. The Industrial Revolution stormed in. Antagonistic class structures emerged, paced off from each other, and clashed in the struggle that Marxists thought would be the end of capitalism.

I want to think back in this essay on how in the 1940s the class struggle determined the life of a young, middle-class westerner like me, caught in his class and locked off from the privilege enjoyed by his betters. I want to reflect on that struggle and its impact on fishing. I want to try to trace how this class struggle and national experience in the end turned out to favor people like me, those of us born on the wrong side of the tracks,* but who, paradoxically, have been sustained and inspired by the grand tradition of classical, upper-class angling.

I recall how, after being discharged from the navy at the end of World War II, what with its great social leveling effects, I and my friend Alan Olson enjoyed baiting the estimable angling entrepreneur Hank Roberts, who was to do so much for egalitarian western fly fishing. In our cultural confusion and immaturity, we baited Roberts with the snobbery of half-baked ideas that we had gleaned about eastern fly-fishing practices and tackle. When Hank, in his thriving new Boulder, Colorado, company, prophetically proclaimed "Western Tackle for Western Fishermen" and began its manufacture, Al and I smarted off with what we thought were the virtues of eastern angling that we little understood. But still, to our credit, we sensed an essential characteristic of the *gentle* life: that it was always lived closely with sport and the spirit of sport. It had elegance and we were envious.†

That gentle angling life on the *right* side of the social-economic tracks in northeastern America, especially in and around New York, took as its model the highly class-stratified social and angling structures of Great Britain, where the angling world divides between *game* fishing for trout and salmon for the privileged and *coarse* fishing in slow, warmer waters for fish we call "rough," for common sorts of people. This division of sport is of ancient provenance. When hunting and gathering ceased to be the principal economy, humankind turned to agriculture on established demesnes and moved inexorably toward feudal economic and social structure based on ownership of the land by the few and the indenturing of the many who only worked the land they did not own. The pattern was set. Sports of field and stream also belonged to the owners, the privileged, the nobility, not to the likes of me.

In the seminal 1496 *Treatyse of Fysshynge wyth an Angle,* the author declares in no uncertain terms that a central purpose of the *treatyse* is to keep this important learning about fishing, especially fly fishing, from falling into the hands of ordinary folks, who could not possibly be morally or ethically worthy of it. The tracks were laid out from the beginning.

As land was the basis of class and privilege in Britain, on this side of the Atlantic money, preferably *old money,* old wealth, was the lodestone of the upper class. Old money enriched by generations of inheritance, privilege, and breeding, of manners and leisure and tradition, but always that *money* that dare not speak its name became the *code of class.* The select and fortunate few somehow understood, deep in their marrow bones, that they deserved their wealth and privilege—never mind that big chunks of it often were earned through ruthless exploitation, even fraud.

We know that today's golf links, the poor relation of field and stream, are often the site of business deals large and small, that out there money is the talk of the town—right up front. But that was not so in the salmon camps or trout clubs of the past, where direct, open dealing was never quite proper, not good manners, not part of the *code.* Money and dealing were doubtless in the *atmosphere* of camp and clubhouse, but only as a *climate,* resulting in associations that once back in town could be welded into hard-and-fast deals.

This all-powerful moneyed class made up the membership of the elegant and influential angling and social fraternities. Their gentleman members had graduated from the best schools with their gentlemen's degrees. Many achieved the manner of the educated if not the intellectual prowess. They were, though, the captains of industry and business, surrounded socially by their close associates and guests—often celebrities from publishing, the academy, arts, and fashion—even occasional European lesser nobility of broken fortunes—whom they kept in tow for the distinction and tone that might rub off on them and their clubs and camps. Not infrequently they admitted their wives, some of whom even fished.

Many of these leaders in the world of finance and its affairs may have lacked broad culture themselves, but many of them, at the same time, understood the role of high culture in the life of their class and were willing to pay for its support.

If these "captains" lacked vast holdings of land as such, they sought to behave as though, like their British cousins, they held what they had as an *estate*, with ancestral overtones of ancient right. If they were to farm, to use their land productively, they made certain that they were seen to be doing it as gentlemen and ladies.

They understood how to use servants and live surrounded by them—how to be waited on and at the same time to know that their secrets were largely transparent to those they employed to dote on them. Wasn't it a fair trade-off for having someone to carry out their slops? Might not this be a metaphor for the whole class idea: that being a member in good standing, *one did not have to deal with one's own slops?*

These spectacular and substantial people knew the code of class and privilege and understood its importance. They observed its responsibilities when they could—otherwise how should they maintain their authority over the rest of us?

Their domestic lives were a far cry from ours on our side of the tracks. While our cellular families were jammed tight together amid all the sordid tensions of daily life, the "better" sort of people lived in a more *spacious* manner. Members of the great families, for better or worse, might go their own luxurious ways, enjoy a highly individual leisure, and remain almost private in their intimate affairs. The head of the family might, for instance, spend an entire summer in a salmon camp if so inclined. Leisure was a conscious and cultivated "art." One was obligated to have lots of it and to do it well.

From our wrong side of the tracks we may have sneered at

those elegant rich folks, at *the carriage trade,* the *swells,* the *hoity-toity,* but they knew what they were doing. While there was agitation in the labor movement to make us aware of the extent to which big money interests depended on our poor money interests and on our *labor,* we were slow to realize and understand it. We were producing their wealth—and all too pacified in our doing it.

The nobs controlled the best fishing—the great Canadian salmon rivers and the best water on the best northeastern American rivers and streams. We could never have afforded that fishing, could not have behaved properly on that water if we had had access. On our side of the tracks, we didn't even know how to dress properly for our sport. Today's breed of TV bass fishermen in their bass boats prove it. They are the extreme expression of our *nobodyness,* if not our vulgarity.

Generally speaking, the privileged and powerful anglers tried to be as good custodians and stewards of their waters and fish as they could or knew how. Lumbering was the bane of the salmon rivers; industrial pollution from the tanneries was a constant threat to trout fisheries like the great Brodheads. Those in control of the waters did what they could in view of the irony that the degradation of their rivers resulted from the very *Big Business* that was the source of their fortunes and ideology.

These American aristocrats were the custodians of the *high style* in angling for which we *nobodies* remain forever wistful. This grand style began in a proper, restrained behavior, integral to the code. The style insisted on the aesthetics and traditions of sport over innovation and technology. One might, for instance, cast for days over a run of salmon with never a hit yet preserve a decorum to be rewarded at the end of each strenuous day by the consolations of the "good living" back at camp,‡ an evening of fine food and liquors, good conversation, and *books,* the rich angling literature, some of which they themselves had inspired and fostered.

But they were doomed.

In the end, we nobodies won out! We who fished the wrong side of the tracks for trout, bass, and panfish wherever they were to be found—and in any way necessary. No purists we! In America's dual angling culture, democracy carried the day—which is to say that egalitarianism prevailed over highly centralized and powerful privilege. Even the wide American manufacture of affordable, practical, and replaceable tackle, beginning in the early nineteenth century, played a role in this move toward democracy in sport. History was switching sides.

For one thing, the national wealth greatly increased and at the same time was much more widely disbursed. As the nation grew in the second half of the twentieth century, there were simply more men and women in control of business, industry, the academy, publication, and the arts. There were many more "important" people with more money and more power than ever before. If a minor corporate executive could now afford to rent a rod for two weeks on the Miramichi or join a club on the Beaverkill, he became an immediate threat to those decently landed squires of the sport who tried to hold tight to the entire river. It was the beginning of the end, the breakup of *estates* into merchantable fishing beats for rent. The demotic bourgeoisie were on the march on a worldwide stage.

For another thing, World War II happened. A great cultural and social leveler, the war almost overnight let hoards of people like me into the promise of the good life. The GI Bill converted myriads of us into the *new professionals* who rebuilt intellectual, scientific, and technological America. We were the new professionals but without the polish, standing, or associations of the "real thing" that we were to displace. We were exactly the rude, upstart, unwashed element that Harvard College so feared would arise and despoil traditional American values if a veterans' educational rights bill should pass the Congress. The old professionals were the comfortable pals of the rich and privileged, but we parvenus had no clear idea yet of who we were, nor any idea of how to behave if we had known. We only wished that we, too, could live the angler's life in style.

The ace up our sleeve was *technology*—that democratic anybody's land where we could all scratch and feed. Al McClane's superb writing on technology and technique in fishing after the war gave us the chance of becoming a new class with our own distinction as anglers. The new science and attendant technology, in a clean sweep, obscured style and aesthetics in angling as it did the rest of late-modern life. The classic fourteen-foot, two-handed salmon fly rod had always been a right rod to use because it was a *correct* rod to use. That was the way things were! But not when a four-ounce, ten-foot carbon rod could pitch the new flies just as far and easier—and cheaper.

I think that a model moment may have come in 1943, when Lee Wulff (Alaska born, by the way), in what became almost a media event, killed a fine salmon with the use only of a reel and line—no rod at all. It was a technical tour de force that proved much about the dynamics of fishing tackle. But looked at from another angle, it was unwittingly a *rude* gesture. It threw the slops of generations of superb anglers and their way of life right back in their faces. Wulff went on to kill salmon with one-piece, six-foot fly rods of scarcely more than an ounce or two in weight. It, too, was, in a sense, an affront to the tradition that had bred him.

The built-wing salmon flies of George Kelson and his successors in the Gilded Age that were thought essential to the sport got watered down with hair wings and radically reduced parts. Even George La Branche's great work with the dry fly for salmon must take its share of blame for the breakdown of the greater tradition of fly fishing for salmon. (Call it "progress" if you will, but progress has yet to be identified by anyone as a primary value in angling.)

And then the revolution in transportation: anglers of every economic persuasion could now get anywhere on the fishing globe quickly. This new ease and economy of travel began with the advent of the great railroads, which pointed the angler's interest away from the East to "out West," with all its romance and great fishing opportunity. Today air travel can easily get us to a quick weekend in an Alaskan salmon camp, to the sea trout of Argentina, or to Arctic Russian salmon and at a price a great many can afford. It's the cultural stampede of the hoi polloi.

I can't get out of mind the occasional practice of the classic salmon fisherman of the past, who, when once he had hooked his fish and enjoyed its first run and a leap or two, handed the rod over to his guide to do the donkey work of getting the fish to the gaff. In such might lie the spirit of the privileged, the difference between them and me, the haves and the have-nots. In a little-known but important French symbolist drama, *Axël,* by the aristocrat Villiers de l'Isle-Adam, the protagonists Axël and Sara plan their ecstatic suicide rather than stain their love with coarse, worldly life—with their slops, as it were. Axël says to Sara, "As for living, our servants will do that for us."

Yes, those servants and those *fishing guides* would land their masters' fish, keep their secrets, and carry their slops—generally living the coarseness out of their masters' lives. They knew their place and their business. Today's servants, today's guides, seem to want to be our buddies! It's called democracy.

I want to suggest a recent film as perhaps the best way to experience and understand these cultural tensions of class and their possible resolutions. Robert Altman's film *Gosford Park* (2002) renders all that I'm struggling with here in words in the most brilliant cinematic terms. The film might be thought of as a rich seriocomic analysis of the last weekend of the English class system and the beginning of the late-modern mess.

If one would experience the *idea of money* as it was among the privileged classes, he has only to see the actor Kristin Scott

Thomas as the weekend hostess react to the American film director's remark (he's clearly from the other side of the tracks) that though he must use the telephone to talk to Hollywood, he will reverse the charges. Ms. Thomas makes it clear in a stunning speechless little gesture of shock followed by revulsion that he has just said something profoundly dirty: he has mentioned money in *her* home.

So, the grand manner is nearly dead and gone. What, then, are we left with of the greatness of our angling tradition, of that grand manner?§ What have we to remind us of what once was, even though we had no personal experience of it? Of course we have its literature, but I think the current enthusiasm for the Imperial Victorian salmon fly might be one emblem or memorial of the tradition. Tyers tie them, collectors collect them, historians study them, and we all stand in awe of them. As talismans, they remain to gather in memory.

There is also our profound nostalgia for a past of angling elegance, style, and tradition—to the manner born. Witness the books and articles currently trading on that nostalgia. Think of the fascination many young and serious anglers today find in waving around a fourteen-foot Spey fly rod, little understanding that it is very like the salmon rods of our betters who went before us. Good old things, seemingly lost, tend to return and compel our interest.

Me, I like to go a-peeking across the tracks, to the other side of the towns of our fishing, hoping to learn their secrets and lore and that some of their ancient polish and tradition might rub off on me. I need constantly to feed my snobbery in order not to feel, even in my old age, entirely feckless.

The irony in all this "democratic," mostly western development is that we, the *technocrats,* now in the vast majority, have carried the day. But now, in our discontent, those who can afford it appear to be repeating the sins of the "fathers" in their search of fine and special waters and associations that they too can privatize for their exclusive use. Many are buying up lands at full tilt, in imitation of that upper class of anglers who understood so well the idea of exclusivity, superiority, and privilege.

As the saying is, If you can't beat 'em, join 'em. But it remains to be seen if this new *synthetic* upper class, as did those who went before, can grow the romance, tradition, style, and aesthetic that all fine fishing deserves—and not merely divide fishing once again with tracks running between a parvenu, enronic "upper crust" and us ordinary folks.

*On the wrong side of the tracks, largemouth bass are the most sought after of freshwater fish. For those on the other side, the more stylish smallmouth alone justified working the warmer waters. But American warm-water fishing was always too good to ignore. We took it to our hearts on this wrong side of the tracks and made much of it, even gave it a literature.

†See *Meditations on Hunting,* by the Spanish philosopher José Ortega y Gasset (New York: Scribner's, 1972), p. 31 and *passim,* for the most probing analysis of the role of hunting, and by extension field sports, in both aristocratic and ordinary life.

‡Some camps may indeed have been rustic *tent* camps, those pushed far upriver into the near wilderness. Otherwise salmon camps were, rather, *lodges,* comfortable, with every amenity other than modern plumbing, that money could buy and trains, wagons, and boats transport to the "civilized" reaches of the rivers.

§The first two chapters of Ernest Schwiebert's *The Henryville Flycasters* (Far Hills, N.J.: Meadow Run Press, 1998) provide an intimate look into the early life and times of this "better" class of anglers on Pennsylvania's Brodheads. I've heard it suggested that Schwiebert's *Chronicle* of Henryville and the Brodheads is a deft effort to place the tradition of the lower Poconos on a footing with that of the Catskills in the history of American fly fishing. Schwiebert suggests that William Cowper Prime, in his noted *I Go A-Fishing* (1873), lays down the essentials of the *code* that would come to control privileged sport. Reading Schwiebert one gathers, also, that a dependable sign of the privileged angler is his having fine, vintage wines never out of reach.

A SCARY LITTLE STORY

For the waters are come in unto my soul.
I sink in deep mire, where there is no standing:
I am come into deep waters, where the floods overflow me.
—Psalm 69

The thin mud turned quick in a slough I was trying to cross in a bend of the Madison River in Yellowstone Park. I began going straight down. When the muck reached my upper chest, I threw my rod to solid ground, hoping that my friends would find it and know where I had gone down. At the same time a gallery of spectators, a dozen or more, gathered on the road above to watch what I was sure were my last moments. No one came to help, though I yelled for it. When the mud reached my chin, my feet hit something solid and gave me a push up to begin a slow struggle to the surface, where I was able to lie prone on the muck and roll myself to safety a few yards away. As I lay there exhausted but glad to be alive, one of my audience up on the road called out, "You ought to be more careful."

CEOs and Fly Fishing

AN ARTICLE IN USA TODAY DEALS AT LENGTH with the phenomenon of executives and CEOs of big business and corporations turning to fly fishing. This comes as no surprise to those interested in the sociology of our sport, but the depth and size of the article suggest that something significant is going on, not just in fly fishing, but in corporate culture itself. The author writes from a curiously pre-enronic innocence, as though nothing much were happening these days to the CEOs he has interviewed beyond their taking up the fly rod in their off-hours. He makes it sound almost idyllic:

> Many CEOs speak of fly-fishing as being more Zen-like than business-like. The river's roar is the opposite of a golf course. Shop talk is impossible, thereby enabling complete focus on the complexity at hand. CEOs say it clears their mind and frees them of stress.*

Okay, but it's what the writer is *not* saying that interests me more—especially the implications of that last sentence about *stress*.

I've long thought and argued that *fishing is fishing* whether by rod, net, spear, trap, or hand line, and I hold on to that. But I'm now forced to consider the possibility of a larger range of motivation and reason behind fishing among certain constituencies.

The *USA Today* article speaks of the ways in which the character and talents of an executive, the qualities that make her a crack chief executive, may also be what can make her a fine and devoted fly fisher. Many business moguls feel that they meet a significant challenge in facing off a trout with a fly. They are doing something that they can get really good at, like management, and go to the top. The implication is that fly fishing is a hotshot sport because hotshots find it compelling and want to spend considerable time, energy, and money doing it.

The newspaper's analysis reads all open and aboveboard—at first. Soon, though, when one mulls it over a little, an underground of meaning begins to appear, in spite, I'll wager, of the author's intentions.

Many high-pressured people in high places have turned to fly fishing in mid- or even later life because, they say, they are looking for an appropriate outlet for their energies and skills. They are typically overachievers, restless, and . . . and what? I've a hunch that down deep they are restless, stressed, and *desperate.* It may well be a clinical response to the desperations and depredations of postmodern American professional business life, where meaning, purpose, and value are in question. It becomes an *existential* question.

The question is powerfully dramatized in Henrik Ibsen's *Peer Gynt,* in which the antihero Peer, who has coursed the entire world and come up empty-handed, ends up a heap of despair and wonders just who he is, what he is. In his bewilderment he sits deconstructing an onion. Layer of onion after layer of onion comes away, Peer feeling certain that at the core, the center, the true nature of the bulb will be revealed to him.

But there is no core, no center, just layer after layer receding into meaningless infinity. Just like, he realizes to his horror, his own wretched life. He has no center, no core, no identity. Panic! What to do? Where to turn with the onion now at minus zero?

To fly fishing, perhaps?

Peer, like our CEOs, has been to the top only to discover, to paraphrase Gertrude Stein about Oakland, that "there's no *top* there when you get there"—only the great void.

Well, not quite . . . that terrible *aggression* in the soul remains. What can be done with *that*? Is fly fishing a therapy? Might it be the longed-for sublimation of aggression and the possibility of calm amid all the stress of postmodern madness? It may well be a search for a place of *meaningful action (casting a fly) within a refuge—a retreat out of danger in which to hide.*

The climate of top-management life today must be one of pathological anxiety about stalking indictments and disgrace, even of jail—to say nothing of arriving in the Oakland of Achievement to find that there is no top of the pile there to rest upon after all.

The luxurious consolations of pre-enronic wealth and status have suddenly disappeared. Instead many CEOs face the specter of guilt and criminality.

One can't but think of the robber barons of the nineteenth century. . . . At least we think of them as having style, the Grand Manner of privilege and old wealth. Our fiscal manipulators of today look small in comparison but no less dangerous to the common weal.

I think that the CEO angler may well be a different kind of angler, if not engaged in a new kind of fishing. Think of Izaak Walton's indictment of those Puritan, moneygrubbing London businessmen of the seventeenth century that he warned against in his *Compleat Angler*, how he feared they would storm out of London and take over his beloved River Lea, turning that gently pastoral world into a sty of urban greed and repression. Walton would have both despised and pitied them—as, I suppose, must we.

In our time, what a different breed our new millennium captains of industry anglers are from those who have angled from childhood, who grew up nearly a century ago, at first, maybe, with a willow pole! But with no ax to grind about anything, expecting nothing from fishing beyond its obvious and ancient pleasures. Never would they have expected fishing to be a therapy or a sublimation of their personal and professional problems. How easy and gentle was the old-time angler's progress from pole to rod!

So, maybe there are two *casts of the fly* today, two modes, two motives for the cast. First, and now clearly in the ascendance, is that with the carbon rod, with its sharp, fast, aggressive power stroke that more resembles *attack* than *delivery*—the appropriate cast for a world of war and rumors of war. The other is the older cast, the cast of *delivery*—from a rod of cane, slower, gentler, and easier—the way of the boy with the cane pole, the memorial way he brought forward with him through the years.

If these differing casts are allowed as an analogy, I needn't spell out on which side our CEOs appear to stand. I needn't spell out how different in *spirit* are these casts or how differently they *mean*.

My hunch is that the CEOs as a breed are searching in desperation, not for a *reinforcement* of what they are already good at, but rather *relief* from it, relief from that which led to their panic, from their terrible stress—and the morbidity of their guilt. Perhaps they long for the sort of angling that tradition and lore tell them used to prevail—once upon a better time. We have to hope, for all our sakes, that it's never too late to start a new life, putting the awfulness of one's old life away, but it is always possible, sorry to say, to be quite tardy.

*Del Jones, "Fly-Fishing Hooks the Elite Among Execs," Denver Post, June 24, 2002, p. 4C.

Walking North with Walton

Driving the Peloponnese in Greece some years ago, through that countryside of Arcadia—where myth and tradition locate the Golden Age of pastoral perfection—I looked everywhere for a landscape where shepherds and shepherdesses might tend their flocks under endlessly blue skies, in endless leisure, along crystal brooks, singing their songs of love and peace, with strife and greed unknown and every need effortlessly satisfied. But I could not find it.

When I reread in Izaak Walton's *Compleat Angler* how he walked for miles north out of London to Tottenham and on toward Ware along his beloved River Lea to fish with companions of the stream, when I realize how he urges me, his reader, to take up my bed and walk out to a countryside of lovely little rivers, gentle fields, intimate village inns, and charming country folk, removed from every stress, anxiety, greed, resentment, and ingratitude, when I understand that he offers me that perfection of the rural life in contrast to the deformations of London's mercantile nightmare of viscous moneygrubbing, I just cannot do it.

In our terrible times, we observe the world through a different system of lenses from those of the pastoral. We think we see more clearly and truly and are disabused of Arcadian and Waltonian idealisms.

Thing is, I suspect that the poets of Arcadian perfection and Walton himself knew well enough that the pastoral ideals of Greek myth and of rural Old England were just that: ideals only. But then, an ideal is never *only* an ideal.

Ideals have life and energy of their own. They can live powerfully inside us. They can cause us to try to live in certain ways.

If Izaak Walton's ideal or idea of pastoral angling on the Lea or on the Dove in Derbyshire never quite existed, it surely lived inside his head and heart as it can do in ours—*if we can get it there.*

How *do* we get it? I've not seen it for sale in any fly shop. We may, however, be able to catch it, like a virus, from another angler who has it, as that fellow Venator caught it from Walton himself in the *Compleat Angler*. Or maybe it will rub off from its archetypal memory in art of all kinds. Maybe we are smart enough to invent it for ourselves out of the combination of deep memory and experience. Perhaps we can dream it.

This *idea,* once locked in, *completes* us as *angler*—the *compleat* angler whom Walton called "contemplative." After we have acquired every item of tackle, every angling skill imaginable, this idea, this ideal, calls us to try to live without greed and avarice or morbid striving—a life in harmony with the ideal landscape of the stream itself. A place to be quiet and grateful—and as Walton added, to "go a-angling" and "study to be quiet."

If this ideal was just that, only an ideal, a literary construct from the deeply engaged Walton, if it never did and never will precisely exist, if there are no landscapes of that perfection, if it was all a matter of Walton's all-creating artistic and social imagination, it was for him, nevertheless, an instrument of his moral and psychological salvation. How terribly urgent, then, must it be for us now, in our awful predicament, to imagine that ideal as powerfully as we can and *act it out.* We need rescue—from ourselves.

It's Only Fly Fishing

I will not forget the doctrine which you told me Socrates taught his Scholars, that they should not think to be honored so much for being Philosophers as to honor Philosophy by their virtuous lives. You advised me to the like concerning angling, and I will endeavor to do so; and to live like those many worthy men.
—Venator, on the last page of Izaak Walton's
The Compleat Angler

THERE I WAS SITTING QUIETLY BETWEEN these two fly-fishing luminaries, who got into a duet on the theme: "It's only fly fishing." They were eager, in their constitutional modesty, to deny special worth to a life-in-fishing as though, if they had chosen surgery, they might have been more worthy people. They wanted to go on record as unwilling to put fly fishing alongside the professions as a measure of the worthy life.

The longer I listened, the more uneasy I became.... Here they were, trying their best to deny that their particular interest in life and work, fly fishing, amounted to anything very much after all. Without saying so in as many words, they were *ranking* the values of human enterprise and consigning themselves to a lowly place in that ranking.

I suppose that when I was young, I might have been tempted to rank the professions, to think that some sorts of enterprise were nobler than others, *that the finer professions made for finer people*. But now in my old age that's impossible to believe. I look about me and conclude that the profession does not make the person. In fact, it's the other way around.

Of course there are those notoriously bad people who have excelled in their work and changed the world for the better—or the worse, but for most of us the value of a profession, of a life's work, is the quality of the particular life that a person *expresses through that work*.

Some will hold that those professions that serve other people should be most highly esteemed, and so they arrive at a ranking. But as there are many ways to skin a cat, so there are many ways to serve. Ranking them as to value is doubtful. Values are, after all, only what human beings, in their radical inspirations, synthesize in order to maintain a culture.

So, let's not say, "It's only fly fishing"; rather, let's say, "It's only human life." Saint Augustine taught that "we all stand in the same condemnation." All we poor devils can do, then, in this generally sordid situation of ours, is to try to live as full, rich, and useful a life as we possibly can—whatever it is we do to get our groceries.

Song of the Forebears
SING:
Aelian-Berners and Dennys.
Mascall-Barker and Markham.
Taverner-Franck and Venables.
Walton and Cotton.

Bowlker-Ronalds-Pulman and Stewart.
Francis-Blacker and Ogden.
Mottram-Marryat-Halford and Skues.
Bethune-Herbert-Phillipe and Norris.

Henshall-Marbury-Green.
Gordon-La Branche-Harding and Rhead.
Hewitt-Stevens-Knight and Harris.
Bergman and Flick-Jennings and Bates.

Kelson-Hills-Price Tannant and Cross.
Leisenring-Darbee-Marinaro and Fox.
Atherton-Hogan-Brooks and Wulff.
Leonard-Payne and Edwards.

Granger-Weber and Herter.
Trueblood-Haywood and Carhart
MacDonald-Ritz and McClane.
Middleton-Haig Brown-Bailey and Roberts.
SING THEM All!

Nativism
The Call for Species Cleansing

WHEN IN 1952 THE GREENBACK CUTTHROAT TROUT, that elegant native of Colorado's South Platte and Arkansas River watersheds, was found still existing, not extinct after all, no one much cared or even was interested. Cutthroat stood in relatively low esteem in the angler's ranking of trout species. We were a rainbow and brown-trout culture with brook trout filling in around the edges. We grudgingly approved the cutthroat for its looks and for its eating, but for little else.

A quarter of a century had to pass before the ideology of *nativism* rose to full cry among the new environmentalists and ecologists who preached the gospel of the 1960s "nature sensibility" on street corners and in curricula across the land.

When by the 1990s it was possible to reestablish the greenback, Colorado was willing to do just about anything for this now glamorous trout and made it the state fish. Suitable habitats were found in which to foster pure and safe-from-hybridization populations. And they were successful. The angling public was generally enthused.

Nativism was an idea whose time had come. Trout Unlimited and the U.S. Fish and Wildlife Commission embraced the concept to the point that they began to speak of rainbows and browns as "exotics" and deemed them undesirable and harmful to native fishes and their waters—not so much to native salmonids as to the family of large minnow fishes native to the Colorado River Basin. There were and are those who wanted to scour our rivers clean of those "exotics," so avid were they in their dedication to the dream of a restored pre-European West.

If this ideology of nativism found comparatively easy going in Colorado, not so in Montana, where at this writing a controversy boils about Upper Cherry Creek flowing through Ted Turner's immense domain. It turns out that Upper Cherry Creek in southwestern Montana is one of the best of habitats for a pure strain of the now much-admired west slope cutthroat. There is no doubt but that this native fish is in trouble, losing the battle for survival against both rainbows and browns. To face up to the problem, Turner has promised $343,350, almost the total sum required to poison out all non-native fishes that swim there and make a safe haven for the west slope trout.

But Turner's offer and the plan itself have raised all kinds of hell among the angling and environmental constituencies. Opposition to Turner's initiative has been furious among many anglers. They fear that this is but one more step in the process of evicting them from their rightful waters. Their rhetoric has often been violent in the extreme, Turner taking his lumps in no uncertain terms.

On the other side, there are those in the ranks of the environmentalists who have let fly a destructive rhetoric all their own. One leading editor of a leading fishing magazine, in support of the Turner project, has referred to rainbow, brown, and brook trout as "mongrel," "alien," "*weed*" fish.* Those content to fish for rainbows and browns in "degraded habitats" he likens to sports content with something like "bowling." Only for those, he says, who seek "wild" fish in "pristine" habitat can angling be "meaningful" and the angler "a participant in nature instead of being just a taker."

I know well enough what we can expect in any controversy with indigenous redneckism, the sort opposing Turner: and there's little we can do about it. But there is something to be said about those, like our leading editor, who presume to be on the side of the angels and have theory and practice on their side. They ought to know better. Still, they think and speak an environmental violence all their own. In the end, they propose a phony romanticism of both biology and sport.

It must surely be a wonderful thing to discover a still existing species once thought to be extinct. It must surely be an almost equally wonderful thing to have the power to protect a threatened species. It's hard to imagine how a person could not become devoted to a subject species over which she has something of the power of life and death. The giant minnows of the Colorado, the greenbacks of the Platte country, the westslopes of western Montana: all arouse this generous devotion.

What is in question, it seems to me, is how we, who count ourselves on the right side of issues like these, see ourselves, how we explain ourselves as savers-of-species. Where do species as *species* fit into the evolutionary scheme of things? Where, in fact, do we humans fit?

Too often we imagine that we are doing nature's own work when we work to preserve species. To use our editor-in-question's language, we imagine that we are "participants in nature."† The truth of the matter is, however, that nature cares nothing at all about species. Species in limitless number have come and gone from the beginning of life on the planet. Individual members of a species live in order to procreate—even to *hybridize*, if need be, in order to survive, and that's all. The survival of a given individual may as readily weaken as strengthen the genetic character of the species in this ruthlessly grand evolutionary mechanism.

Hybridization is integral in the evolution of species. We humans, from our beginnings, literally have lived off the fruits of hybridization in the plant kingdom—to say nothing of the "improvement" of member species in the animal kingdom. Nature does not do its work by protecting the purity of species. Such is not a principle of nature. Nature keeps open its mechanisms for ceaseless, *valueless* change.

Where do we get the idealization of species purity? Not from any models in nature. The idea comes in good part from a highly peculiar, revolutionary *human* trait or capacity, a truly radical process in the universe: *the aesthetic sense.* A population of pure-strain westslopes is to us *a beautiful thing.* The *idea* of such a population is to us beautiful, having its origin in the radicalism of the *human imagination.*

The political reinforcement of the idea comes from our deeply *conservative reluctance* to give up what we have long known. As humans we both invite and resist change and accordingly cast our votes.

From this exclusively human imagination of the beautiful, from seeking its examples and making more of them, comes the act of conceiving *values.* In all the universe, it is we humans alone who constitutionally move through an initial act of the imagination, to the discovery and making of objects and ideas of aesthetic quality, which teach us, in turn, what to value—what to save—in our lives. It's an *unnatural* process.

I won't venture into the perils of a definition of beauty here, trusting the reader to understand that the word does not, of course, mean merely "pretty" but rather special characteristics abiding within a circuit of values that the initial act of *imagination of the beautiful* first set in motion.

We ought not, therefore, to think that when we protect the westslope cutthroat in western Montana that we are the agents of nature's purpose. Rather, we are just another species, albeit an emotionally and intellectually restless one, with this rarest of attributes, the imagination, stumbling our way through our evolution to the point where we invent this crazy, beautiful notion of the value of species. *Nativism is an aesthetic concept.* It may be argued that the notion is itself "natural" because we are fully involved in nature, and therefore whatever we do is a part of nature. But all our notions of value are the *outcome of the process of our evolution* and are eccentric to it.

We have only to think for a moment to remember that the idea of species purity can be a hideously dangerous idea—as well as a lovely one when it's *trout* we're talking about. *Species* purity and *racial* purity go intellectually and politically hand in hand, too often toward monstrous crime—against life itself. It has, in our time, been called *cleansing.*

We can comfort ourselves that our interest in the minor issue of small populations and locations of cutthroat trout is innocent enough in the grand scheme of things. We have not even gone so far as to raise the issue of pure strains in rainbows, browns, and brooks. So far we seem to know when and where to stop.‡

In the end, though, we have to come down off our high horse and realize that when we mess with species, we are not doing nature's work nor are we acting on behalf of what we think are nature's values. We have to keep telling ourselves that nature has no values; only we have them. It is we humans who have invented and introduced them into the nature immediately around us.

Evolutionary biologists are quick to tell us that there is no guarantee at all that the human imagination and its proclivity for the idea of value is or will be successful in the long haul of life on the planet. Values are no more than quirks or byproducts of evolution produced out of an even quirkier thing, the imagination. But it's nevertheless a glorious thing, this imagination, worth living and dying for. It enables us humans to enjoy both the actual world around us and a *virtual* world of the inner life in which to be conscious of ourselves and of the universe. And in it all, one of our grandest secrets is that we all want to *play!* In the spirit of imaginative play we can create a place within ourselves, and in community with others, to rejoice in life and even conceive a safe place for the westslope cutthroat.

But at the same time, we need to grant a proper and generous place to all those hybrids of water, land, and air. We need to honor them in our play and be extremely careful how we puff ourselves up with such unfortunate language as *weed* and *mongrel.* Weeds and mongrels are opportunists like ourselves and have, in their way of life, the future of life itself.

*Ted Williams, "Why Fly Fishermen Hate Ted Turner," Denver Post, April 7, 2002, p. E1.

†Shakespeare's *A Winter's Tale,* Act IV, scene iv, lines 70–108.

‡Boulder, Colorado, enjoys a highly vocal political lobby to protect the rodent prairie dog. It is hard not to believe that this is because the prairie dog has an appealing way of standing erect that can only be described as "cute." It boasts big brown eyes in a handsome, intelligent face. It is readily seen and enjoyed along roads and highways, where it stands up staring back at the observer—and in broad daylight. Everything about the prairie dog suggests that it satisfies the *aesthetic sense,* which the nocturnal gray scavenging rats in our alleys do not. The prairie dog has "Disney" appeal.

A PLAINTIVE NOTE

In the old days we were expected to fight a fish gracefully, carefully, handsomely, until the fish gave up. We regarded with utter disdain those who "horsed in" or "pine treed" their catch. Now that's all changed. They tell us that, for the fish's sake, we are to horse in our fish as fast as possible, with no regard for the aesthetics of the fight. We are told of the buildup of toxic wastes in the fish's flesh if it is overtired. (Is that what happens to me when I get bushed?)

If the aesthetics of conquest are irrelevant, why don't bullfighters simply shoot their bulls and have done with it? Or *why do they fight them at all!*

Solitude
For All Those with Whom I've Fished

A DISTANT AND SOLITARY ANGLER WORKS THE WATER in a vast sepia-toned, full-page, big river scene—an advertisement for Trout Unlimited. The sparse text, only a few words, suggests the age-old sentiment that an angler might well find God out on the river, that being out there is a bona fide substitute for church. The implication is that God is in nature and that nowhere can God be reached on more intimate terms than in an angler's angling. We are urged to believe that fishing is a deeply spiritual experience. Further, we are urged to believe that the more alone, the more solitary we are in our communion with nature, the richer and more abiding will be the experience.

Lying close up against the underbelly of this idea is the idea, an old-time heresy, of *pantheism,* that all nature is suffused with god and, in the next breath, that nature is full of myriad gods: nature gods, a god for most anything and everything. This idea feels good to lots of people.

An uncomfortable division in the consciousness of many a traditional Christian sportsman has been this notion that though one ought to be in church on a Sunday, one can be every bit as worshipful and inspired out fishing. Still, this angler often feels

102

guilty and sneaky about it. Our literature, for instance, contains amusing images of the fisherman of old walking through town, *just possibly to church*, carrying his "walking stick," which walking stick is, in reality, the hollowed-out butt of a long fishing rod. The rod's middle and top joints are secreted away from the prying eyes of the faithful in that hollow butt. The angler is sneaking off to his sport, hoping he won't be caught. If he does get caught, he makes his conventional excuses to the conventionally faithful by declaring that he finds "*his* God" out there on the stream.

I've long assumed that pantheism, the *god-in-nature* idea, is something that people and cultures grow up and out of as soon as they can. Whatever the word *primitivism* may have come to mean today, it suggests pantheism or nature worship. It's a notion that, when it lingers in us moderns, however innocently, is still a sentimentality that for societies and cultures is fraught with danger.

We need to understand that fishing, like Emerson's fringed gentian, is its own excuse for being. It needs no excuses for its appeal. And has little or nothing to do with worship, church, Sundays, religion, or God(s).

But should an angler persist in the idea that fishing is reverential, if not prayerful, and done in the presence of the deity, he will almost certainly insist that he ought to fish alone in order to close the circuit with "his god." And so: *Enter the image of angler angling in solitude.*

I've thought that fishing has not as much to do with solitude, with being alone, as is commonly thought, certainly not as practiced. Izaak Walton, who was as "contemplative" in his recreation and as firmly churched in his religious life as they come, never insisted on angling as solitary. In fact, he appeared to favor the idea of and enjoyed companionship in fishing. Two anglers for him, as for us, remained just the right count.

Two anglers can share everything about their experience, from their lunch to the deepest ruminations on their lives. They validate each other's experience, not the least their fish caught. Two anglers can have a deeply peaceful day. They can tune themselves each to the other. They can look out for each other. They can enjoy the warmth of friendship old and new. And later *they can remember the shared occasion together.*

Let a third angler in and the party gets awkward. Somehow three doesn't work as well. Decisions become complicated. Sharing, uncertain. Intimacy, guarded. Secrets, unsafe. Fishing, like art, tends to be much about keeping secrets, and no secret is safe when a third party gets ahold of it, especially in fishing.

No, I think that the real *solitude of angling* is perfected, not in an angler in lonely isolation, but in the quiet, easy, thoughtful association of *a couple of friends* who can orchestrate their day to the tune of each other's needs and pleasures.

Whenever we want to be strictly alone, we are well advised to be wary of that for which we wish. The solace of solitude can suddenly turn on us and become terrible, unbearable loneliness, even desolation. Who of us hasn't experienced that quick change of the spirit? Working fishermen at sea have always known this awful loneliness and have dreaded it. The darkest, most melancholy, most dangerous, and maybe the hardest of all work is this severe, ancient fishing-as-work. Its transformation into our sporting *play,* into one of the most delightful of pastimes, is a great achievement in human culture.

Nevertheless, we sporting, playing anglers need to remember and honor those *working* fishermen at sea—like those in the book and film *Perfect Storm.* Who of us would want the solitude of those men—and women—out there, so terribly alone, even when they are a crew together?

I think I'm prepared to argue that it's not in our nature to want to be alone.

When anglers say that they want to be alone, I suspect that they mean one of two or three things: first, that they need to be alone on a particularly small piece of water where there is not room for more than one angler at a time—and possibly on secret water at that. Or second, that they have to fish alone in order to meet inflexible time schedules, etc. Or third, that they want to be alone on a particular stretch of water *in order not to be intruded on, butted in on,* by bad-mannered strangers who can make fishing a miserable competition for territory. This is too often the case.

Still, two friends can happily divide up some quite small water and even ward off pushy intruders. I say nothing of the angler like me, who often feels that he ought not to be a drag on another, more vigorous fisherman and spoil his day. Better for me to be out there solo.

As anglers multiply on our limited waters, as anglers are doubled by the shoulder-to-shoulder presence of hired guides, as we may be shouldered out of the way to accommodate this awful commercial invasion, we may, in revenge, cry out for *solitude.* But is that what we *really* want? I think not. Crying out for *solitude* amid extravagant claims for the holiness of nature, for God's or the gods' presence in nature, that we worship there, is neither sound theology nor quite grown-up behavior.

But all's not lost. The best model we have for our sport, which is full of its own "spiritual" nurture, is in that seventeenth-century masterpiece *the Compleat Angler,* when old Walton, on his day of recreation, walks north out of London toward Ware to fish the River Lea, his home stream. With him walks a companion, a friend, the two of them sharing confidences and ideas, their lunch, fishing lore, a midday rest, and the beauties and blessings of the way.

Neither is alone. Each *desires* the other's company. And neither confuses it with going to church—quite another and sterner matter in their lives.

Another Little Story

Bill Woods and I camped at Staley Springs on Henry's Lake, and in the morning, while dawn was still only a possibility, set out among many others in rented rowboats for the big cutthroats famous in that famous lake. The fish hit almost at once on our down-deep flies. Other boats lost in the darkness gave out with grunts of their own steady success.

But we also heard terrible cursing and yelling from what turned out to be a boat with one grown man and two boys who had to have been his sons. The man flailed about uselessly with a beat-up spinning rig and a huge brass spoon, all the while abusing the little boys—in language that made even us blanch. The boys, when we could see them, sat hunkered down and passive, doing their best just to survive.

Eventually, with the sun well up and having caught nothing on his spoon, the man gave up and yelled at the boys to row him in.

At the dock, seated in the stern, he ordered them to get out and secure the boat. Which they did, but with the result that the bow of the little boat tipped up to the sky, dumping the man ass over appetite back into the drink.

All the boats at Staley Springs joined in a great cheer. We rejoiced for those boys—until, that is, we thought of the beating they would probably get later. But for the moment at least, we knew that *poetic justice* was still a possibility.

Caves, Hunters, Paintings, and Reality

A RECENT STUDY OF FLY-FISHING LITERATURE begins by making much of the prehistoric cave paintings of southern France and northern Spain.

It's a commonplace to say that the stunning frescoes of the great beasts of the hunt in those cave paintings of thirty thousand years ago were for the purposes of ritual, sympathetic magic. As mysterious as their origins and uses remain, they may indeed have been thought to possess the power to affect events; that is, to ensure the success of the next day's hunt. (These images could as easily have been of fish and fishing given a marine culture.)

But there is, surely, another, and equally powerful, function of that hunting art, a quite ordinary and basic psychological function that all of us will recognize at once, and that is to excite the hunter, to excite him to imagine the hunt, to plan the hunt, to want to go out and experience its dangers and joys. No actual hunt, though, no fishing trip can ever quite live up to our dream of it as we know it in art, and so it must have been with those early hunters and their wall paintings. The "real" hunt was always doomed to imperfection when compared with that ideal hunt-in-art on the cave walls. The expectation that life is improved by the stimulation of art may be problematic, but it remains irresistible.

Those ancient ancestors, or their shamans, of our aesthetic and sporting life daily took back down into their caves with them their fleeting, ephemeral, even illusory images and memories of their excursion to the outer world, where in danger and desperation they had hunted (or fished) in order to live. Inspired by the immense spreading canvas of those stone walls, they took control, organized their experience, planned strategies, experienced the power of their excitement by representing what they knew and felt in art. They made an alternative reality.

Perhaps today we are better able to understand how those cave paintings worked—as a *virtual* and alternative reality not unlike the encodifications within a computer that allow us to imitate life, to excite and motivate ourselves (or so the industry promises) for a fuller life. Add to the resources of the computer those of magazines, videos, clinics, catalogs, books—fly shops, and we have another entire newly created virtual world of the imagination of immense seductive power.

Is our hanging around in a fly shop of a Saturday morning really very much different from the experience of those caves? Like those primordial ancestors, we hope to live up to our art. But as with those ancestors, the "real thing" is apt to be less than a match for our imagination of it.

Language, image, and symbol do surely drive action or drive us humans *into* action, teach us what can perhaps be done, what we must try to do. Art, then, is at least as much, if not more so, an *incitement to life* as a record of it.

I have argued before that our fishing is the *material expression of our angling literature.* We go from our cave full of books out into the uncertain and shifting streams of what, for want of a better word, we call "reality." We struggle there awhile, accomplish what we can, and return to the cave again for renewed strategy and inspiration.

In the beginning was the word.

Note: Unresolved is the issue of the depth and utter darkness of the caves. The paintings could only have been made by torchlight or small oil lamps. It's difficult to understand how the paintings could ever have been seen by anyone except as dimly lit fragments of the whole. The caves were certainly not large gathering places of Neolithic people. Why, then, did those painters do it? Why did they go down there into that terrible darkness, with so little chance to have their great work seen?

PERFECT STORM

Betty and I went up Boulder Creek yesterday morning and worked our drys over freely rising brooks and rainbows. It was dandy.

Then last night we took in the film *Perfect Storm*, all about commercial fishing for swordfish and the monstrous Atlantic storm that befell the fishing fleet in 1991.

We came home talking about how our morning's trout fishing was exactly like that swordfishing on the killer ocean—in every detail except the terrible intensity, magnitude, and danger of it. Betty even killed two fish and got a hook in *her* hand. Fishing's fishing!

Yes, but Is It Art?

SOMEONE HAS REMARKED THAT FISHING has no real literature. On the face of it, that's a startling position to take, what with the immense amount of writing about fishing in and out of print.* Immense amounts of it, yes. But is it capital-L *Literature?* Is it *art?* Nope. That *someone* was right. We can allow only Izaak Walton's *Compleat Angler* into Literature's "official" cannon of masterworks with any real conviction.

But we can take heart: while some fishing writing is just plain bad and a lot of it banal, some of it is beautiful and touching. I'd argue that there are bits and pieces here and there in that huge body of writing that rise to the level of *art* or close to it. We ought not to fault angling writers for failing to write Literature-as-art. They aren't, and rarely profess to be, artists. They want only to write as well and thoughtfully as they can about the sport that they love or that pays them. They are ordinarily too modest to imagine themselves as artists. Still, they hope to work at a level above journalism, which is to say that they hope to write for more than just the working day, hope that what they have to say will last at least their own brief span.

Artists don't ordinarily write narrowly about "topics" such as angling. They deal with the world as it intrudes upon them from every angle, at any time, in any place—about all that moves them to want or need to write.

Literature-as-art, imaginative Literature, is mostly about sex, death, and the family. Violence is its meat, laughter its balm. Tragedy, comedy, romance, and satire are its classic modes. Life is its dedication, and language is its joy and its truth. Fishing isn't usually found in those categories.

Still, if fishing can once in a while find a niche in any of Literature's poems, stories, and dramas, so much the better. As readers we love to discover such moments.

It's the particular splendor of fishing that its record in print far exceeds in both bulk and quality that of all other sports. There's something strange about it, about fishing, that *requires that it be written about.* There's something about fishing that is somehow incomplete until written about. It's said that no fisherman can make a lasting reputation for himself without *getting into print about it.* It's the most *writerly* of sports.

And there's no harm done that it's not *Literature, not art.*

*William Radcliffe notes that there were 4,484 texts published in English on angling by the year 1920! What must that number be now!

A Principle of Discourse
or Devin's Worm
I've held that anglers should get themselves free from the tyranny of the fly in order, at least occasionally, to get "back to basics," back to where fishing started and where it has its clearest meaning: in bait—a well-drifted angleworm, for instance.

Now here comes Professor Lee Devin of Swarthmore College

to point out, "We who aspire to punditry must cultivate the habit of chasing ideas wherever they lead, clear down to worm fishing if need be."

It's a bit like the famous principle of the medieval English philosopher Ockham, "Ockham's Razor," which warns that

Entities are not to be multiplied beyond necessity.

We are not to risk an overburdened argument, theory, or classification—we must be spare and skeptical in all things, as in our fly boxes, our writing, even our fishing, you name it. And always to remember to apply Devin's Worm.

The Quality of Angling
Going to the Fishes with Saint Anthony

I NEED TO PROVE TO MYSELF THAT I CAN DEFINE THIS THING that is so important to me, this *fishing*. In a way I feel that I have no real right to it unless I can define it. For better or worse I've always wanted definitions but am well aware how a too-mechanical definition can squeeze the very life out of its subject. In any case, it's a risk to be taken, and this is the place and the time to take it.

Any definition of fishing I come up with must avoid the abstraction, intensity, and subjectivity so much in style today. I need to be brief, concrete, and clear. My definition must be specific but still general; it must be self-evident. While it must allow for feeling, it must never foster feeling for its own sake. It must be a definition that anyone can grasp and perhaps find useful.

So, here goes. I barge ahead in the effort to define *the quality of angling*.

The fundamental thing about fishing is *the act of going to the water, to the fish*. That *thing is* as basic as a thing about fishing can get. As Professor Lee Devin has put it, the moment when we've chased a *thing*, an idea, down as deep and as far as we possibly can, to its utter essentials, that's the moment when the angler puts on a worm. At this point, then, I too must put on the proverbial worm.

Whatever else, then, may be the quality of angling, it begins in the act of *going to the water.* And whatever else we can say about ourselves as a species, we must surely say that *Homo sapiens* is the creature who will always go to the water whenever and wherever there's an opportunity. In that, we are incorrigible. We go to oceans, lakes, streams, springs, rivers, and spas, drawn there by powerful and mysterious forces that we little understand, but always in the expectation that we will be restored, if not healed.

We move through our own two native elements of *air* and *earth* toward a third element: *water.* (*Fire,* the fourth element, may represent the rogue factor responsible for those bad fishing days when we better had stayed at home.) Arriving at the water's edge is always a peculiar experience. We can sit by its side and reflect on its depths. We can enter the margins of the water. Some can dive to modest depths to explore that other world. But there's always that uneasiness, that strangeness about it.

However we get into the water, just to splash around or on a technical dive, we are drawn up short because the water is an *other world,* essentially alien, unfathomable, a mystery. However much we may long for the water, we don't belong there. While we may love the water and can't stay away from it, we are never far from the fear of it. It can be destructive in the extreme.

Ah, but we are often instructed that it was from those very waters that we evolved as living creatures. Furthermore, we are told of late that our animal nature developed from the *sponge,* that the sponge in the depths is the origin of every animal!

We know how common is that metaphor of the oceanic depths for our origins, our first home, for our Great Mother. And the more those depths are revealed to us, the more they become a matter of scientific fact, the more mysterious and wondrous they become. It is precisely as with the moon and the failure of the astronauts to demystify it, its beauty and romance, by the least jot or tittle, just because they walked on it. Our universe won't stand still as an object of aesthetic and psychological wonder. Every day of our experience and knowledge of it only increases its intimate hold on us.

The water we fish is always replete with a special power over our imagination and capacity to wonder. The ancients were sure that springs, oceans, and rivers were sacred and were inhabited by deities of miraculous power. We anglers come to the water with similar expectations of the fish that inhabit there.

Fish are unlike the animals of air and earth. Theirs is a realm of being all their own, to fascinate, sometimes even to frighten and endanger us. They outnumber us in their endless variety. They have no need of us as we of them and thus crush our pride. They seem, in their impact upon us, to suggest that our realm in air may be inferior to theirs in water.

Of course there are exceptions. Saint Anthony of Padua, that brilliant young preacher with every good gift of person that nature could bestow, found his brilliant, famous preaching less and less popular among his flock and so fell into a profound depression—until one day he went to the water and preached to the fishes, who came to the surface, where they were glad and excited to hear his homilies.

For us, as for the saint, it's a matter of finding a way to break through that watery surface, that barrier, to the depths beneath, to find whatever it is we feel must surely be there. A fine fish must surely lie in that hole upstream under that protecting rock. Shall I play the saint? Will the fish "hear" my fly or my worm? And come to it?

And so, once we have come to the water, we long to enter into it and experience something of that other realm of being. And there are not a few ways of doing that, of getting into the water, but one of the most ancient and essential is with a magical thread, a line held in the angler's hand as he lets down the other end, baited with the only offering we can imagine, not being saints, *food* for the insatiable appetite of the fish below. The equation is completed in the insatiable appetite of the angler above. The dynamic of the thread of line is between the basic physical need of the fish and the angler's equally basic need. *From belly to belly!*

That's the nature of the contact—or contract; that's the authorization for crossing along the thread of line from one realm, one element, into another. And it's fundamental! Our need to be fed!

The quality of angling, then, at this point in the argument is: *going to the water,* confronting that limpid surface, that profound boundary, in our crisis of physical need and penetrating it, getting through it with the *silken thread* that will allow a negotiation between the bellies of fish and angler.

The quality of angling is, I believe, completed in that word *silken,* which we all readily understand and find evocative. The silken thread that leads what Shakespeare calls "the treacherous bait" to our fish is perhaps the heart of a *total silken technology of angling* that is utterly unlike that in any other sport. The word itself seems almost the very property of fly fishing and not only for leader and line. We speak of our silken flies, of the silken whisper of our cast in the air, the silken mechanism of the reel, the matchless silken feel and decoration of the rod in the hand, even of the air through which it moves, the intricate yet harmonious silken flows of water down the stream: all of it conducing to what I don't hesitate to call *a silken cast of mind in the angler.*

William Herrick, in his *occasional* poem about the burial of the great John Atherton's ashes on the Beaverkill, ends with:

Downstream a fisherman moved silk

In that wonderful image of the cast, one can't but see that it's a silken, sensuous thing that we do, and with this, we come close to defining *angling itself.* We do, like the saint, "talk" to the fish in our own special way. Sometimes I catch myself literally talking out loud to them. Sometimes they appear to listen, and I'm glad.

Once in Padua, in his basilica, I passed by the reliquaries containing the remains of Saint Anthony, one of which was his larynx, with which he formed those words that drew to him the fish of his watery parish. I knew that one day that experience would answer a need of mine. His silken words, that thread of the heart's language, passing through the barrier-surface between air and water to satisfy a need above and below, would be the analogy that I could risk, as analogies are always risky, in my need to define fishing.

So, this is my definition: *The angler goes to the water, to the fish, in a silken consciousness and with a silken line, to pass through the surface barrier, forever expecting to satisfy that need of man and beast to be fed in body and soul.*

REBUKED

After reading the above essay in draft, my wife remarked that she had never felt the need for a definition of fishing.

Where Are the Flies of Yesteryear?
An Essay with Interlinear Commentary

JUST RECENTLY A FRIEND, IN A FINE FIT OF DEVOTION to the past, wondered out loud what had happened to the old flies we had all loved and fished, say, around 1940. Why couldn't we still use them? Wouldn't they be as effective now as they ever were? What happened?

It's a good question.

What happened, I believe, is that the change in trout flies over the past century and a half from presentational artifice to representation of the natural—of which we are all aware—took place as a result of the same historical-cultural pressures and ideas as did the rest of our evolving, sometimes revolutionary, society.

In my last days before going off to World War II, I worried about my flies that had to be put aside for "the duration." I put them in mothballs, tight containers, and every other security I could think of.

Here's a catalog of the old flies from which mine were selected:

Rio Grande King, Western Bee, Captain, Coachman,

Royal Coachman, Lead-winged Coachman, Cowdung,
Blue Bottle, Jock Scott, Silver Doctor, Wickham's Fancy,
McGinty, Greenwell's Glory, Blue Quill, Ginger Quill,
Black Gnat, the Gray Hackles: yellow, red, green, and peacock;
Grizzly King, Gold Ribbed Hare's Ear, White Miller, Yellow
Sally, Badger Palmer, Blue Dun, California Hackle, the
Brown Hackles: peacock, red, and yellow; Flight's Fancy,
Professor, Pink Lady, Mosquito, Montreal, Queen of Waters,
King of Waters, Red Ant, Black Ant, March Brown, Cahills,
light and dark; Rube Wood, Red Ibis, Governor, Parmachene
Belle, Blue Upright, Whirling Blue Dun, Warden's Worry,
Willow, Dusty Miller, Seth Green, Deer Fly, Iron Blue Dun,
Mormon Girl, Mister Mite and family: Sandy, Buddy,
Dina, and Lady—and The Major Pitcher.

When in 1946 I had lived to open up my cache of flies for
the first postwar season, I found them curiously disappointing.
They didn't have the same hold on my imagination as they had
before I went away.

Something new was in the air. Everything seemed on the edge
of change, and my dear old flies looked somehow "old-fashioned,"
though I would then have been hard put to explain why. I could
not have guessed back then what now seems quite apparent to me:
that trout flies and their development came under the same pres-
sures and influences as every other aspect of our lives, that the course
of the trout fly in the twentieth century reflects and parallels the intel-
lectual and cultural history of that tumultuous time.

Many of those flies that I had stored away for "the duration"
were traditional wets because, where I grew up in the West, we
were an old wet-fly culture. Their range, as in the list above, was
considerably more limited than the spectacular array of *national*
wet-fly patterns as in the *painted* plates in Ray Bergman's influential *Trout* (1938). Perhaps, among those hundreds of mostly *fancy* Bergman flies, the Royal Coachman best illustrates the

old-fly *type*. This American development from the Coachman of English origin is a model of the *type* of the conventional "wet fly": all peacock, red, fiery brown, and white, with a tail of various material. It's probably the most famous of all flies in North America and was common to almost every old fly book.

I'd like now to work on this matter of fly *types*, old and new, by suggesting a four-part abstract: *form, material, inspiration,* and *use.* What can we say first of the old order of flies according to these categories?

Form: The flies were traditional and conventional; that is to say, in physical shape they were all pretty much alike and had been around for a very long time, were widely accepted, and bore only incidental connection, here and there, with natural insects.

Material: The flies were tied from what we might call *imperial* stuffs, from all over the world, made possible by the imperial hegemony of Britain and America. These materials were often luxurious, exotic, and expensive—beautiful feathers, furs, and hair for the greater glory of ladies' hats and trout and salmon flies.

Inspiration: The inspirations for these flies were rather more limited: they were *academic* and circumscribed by authority not unlike the control of the great academies in nineteenth-century Europe that sought to protect language, art, and culture from corrupting innovation.

Use, or utility: Their use was reflexive; that is, they had to be useful within the convention, the tradition. Seemingly numberless patterns were invented but *within* the convention, few outside it. The proper use of a proper fly was to be a proper fly.

On this side of the Atlantic, the old flies worked particularly well in the north- and middle-eastern states for the native brook trout, which never—or hardly ever—turned a blind eye on the fancy, the pretty, and the colorful. These flies were part and parcel of *a lingering romantic inspiration.*

*Truth to tell, there were those few staple flies, subversives
in the ranks of the old fancies, which suggested the real
thing by virtue of their subdued and "natural" colors.
They took lots of fish. I'd nominate the Ginger Quill
for a leader in that pack.*

The seeds of change had been planted long before I waded in
after my war. The change had begun, in fact, in the shank of the
nineteenth century and the late romantic period with such pivotal figures as that hard-fishing Scotsman William C. Steward,
who proposed in 1857 that we work upstream to a position behind
or below a fish, out of its line of sight, and cast upstream over it.
Essential to this revolutionary idea was the need for flies of a new
type. And so began the end of the time-honored across-and-
downstream cast-and-drag of old flies inherited from the *Treatyse*
of 1496 and later from Izaak Walton's dear companion Charles
Cotton, down to those of Mary Orvis Marbury and, in the mid–
last century, Ray Bergman.

But fishing, fly fishing especially, has always moved slowly
indeed, cherishing its old ways and resisting the new. It's remarkable how few and how slow have been the fundamental changes
since the first image of rod fishing in a famous Egyptian drawing of 2000 bc (see page 163).

But from the mid-nineteenth century on, something really
new in Western culture and intellectual life was stalking the old
ways of thinking, seeing, and doing. Modernism was stalking
every aspect of our cultural lives. If modernism meant anything,
and it was beginning to mean *everything*, it was to mean a speed-
up in all things, even changes in fly fishing. The full brunt of the
new movement was felt suddenly and with history-changing
force at the "scandalous" Armory Show in New York in 1913. The
radical paintings shown there, which so profoundly shocked the
"academy" and outraged public taste, would change forever how

we would look at and value aesthetic objects, social and political life, even *reality* itself.

> Dadaist painter Marcel Duchamp's infamous and
> wonderful Nude Descending a Staircase tended to sum
> up the experience of the show and incite to near riot.

Nothing would escape modernism's fierce analysis. Not even the trout fly could escape the powerful vortex of its influence.

And following hard upon the Armory Show was World War I, with its unspeakable horror, universal disillusionment, and despair. Young men were forced to put away their flies for the duration of that war too. In England nearly an entire generation of young men were never to see their flies again. In the face of disaster on this scale, something had to change!

Change, both for better and worse, did take place—and fast. Reform of the trout fly like everything else accelerated greatly in the barely thirty years between 1918 and 1948, from the end of one immense war to another. While most anglers, especially out West, in, let us say, 1940, were happily using their heavy gut straps of two reliable old wet flies, out in the greater world, the integrity of those very flies was already being undermined, even before the Great War.

I can only list the most influential of those who changed the fly. Suffice it to say that Frederick M. Halford as early as the 1890s had defined the new floating fly in England. G. E. M. Skues followed Halford, re-imagining the sunk fly and inventing the nymph on the same English waters. Theodore Gordon was doing his important work on the American dry fly in the Catskills, work that others, like Art Flick, would bring to fruition. At midcentury James Leisenring in Pennsylvania was working his own magic on nymphs and wets with precisely selected materials and an acute attention to translucence and texture. Again in Pennsylvania, Vincent Marinaro would do his important work on terrestrial insect patterns and "discover" the *hidden hatch*, the *Tricorythodes*, that would lure us away from our old size 8s, 10s, and 12s, through the smaller 14, 16, and 18s—and most importantly down to size 20, 22, and 24s! This relentless downsizing of our flies was crucial, and its importance cannot be overestimated. The tiny hooks left the old flies stranded.

When I read Marinaro in 1952, I immediately tied some of his size-24 Jassids, took them up the South Fork of the Shoshoni River, and made fools of those browns.

Yet another Pennsylvanian, Ed Koch, came along in the 1960s to tell us how trout feed heavily on minuscule midges. He developed dressings for and promoted them as essential to any well-appointed fly box of the new dispensation. Who would have thought that these wretched little creatures, these inconsequential, annoying midget insects were a primary food for trout! We called them "gnats" in the old days and wanted only to shoo them away.

A decade earlier, artist-angler John Atherton proposed an elegant theory for an effective new series of flies. *Impressionism*—as in French painting—where reflected, not incidental, light was the secret of the brilliant life of those pictures, was the working principle in Atherton's radiant flies.

And in the present moment, John Betts, a leading innovator, has discovered and introduced many remarkable synthetic materials to fly tyers. Their wide and innovative use has brought on immense and exciting changes in fly design.

In general, then, translucent and reflective materials, natural and synthetic, were replacing opaque silks, wools, chenilles, and duck slip wings. Hackles were thinning down to "just enough" (except in some attractor dry flies). Flies were getting "buggier" and more effective.

And not to be overlooked are ultralight, strong nylon tippets down to 8x and hooks down to size 28. They have played a decisive role in the changeover to the new flies.

The old flies, of that now antique *type,* carried within them the seeds of their own demise.* While we continued to fish our tandem two wet flies mostly across and downstream in the old pre-Steward manner, we were slow to realize that the flies themselves were too big, too coarse, often too flamboyant, too often modeled upon prevailing commercial examples—too generally unlifelike for our trout, who were wising up to the old stuff.

I knew a commercial tyer of wet flies back in the 1930s who winged every pattern with duck primary slips and trimmed them into an absolutely regular back-sweep shape. To those of us who knew no better, they looked really neat. And they were two for a quarter.

Those trout, for whatever genetic, evolutionary, behavioral scientific reason, were growing steadily more selective, warier, and more easily put down and required more careful stream tactics from the angler, who could no longer be so casual about fishing. Countless trout were now being caught and released repeatedly, and though they are creatures of "little brain," still they can learn—especially with the constant opportunity to get a lesson from the now endless numbers of us stomping through their riffles.

Some there are who argue that if we would dress the old flies on smaller hooks, dress them more lightly and fish them on lighter tippets, they would still work on selective trout. No doubt but that's true. But no doubt also that those flies tied in that "new" way would be a transformation from the given *type* of old fly headed toward the *new*. When I dress a Rio Grande King on a size-20 hook, it's no longer the same creature as the size 10 I used when I began throwing flies in 1938.

When I was a kid, a neighbor, Nick Shons, was the nemesis of trout in Boulder Creek. He'd take a new Rio Grande King with its white duck quill wing and chew that wing down to a mere nubbin of a thorax ahead of the black chenille body. He'd then chew off a lot of the hackle in the same operation, and my good Lord, did he catch fish on that

*and a yellow-bellied gray hackle! Neither he nor I knew the
first thing about thoraxes and the anatomy of insects.*

While anglers are conservative and slow to change, they
won't reject a killing fly pattern. And so, if evidence is needed
for the demise of the old fly *type*, a peep into the fly boxes of the
contemporary angler or into the endless little compartments of
flies for sale in the fly shops and into the commercial catalogs
will prove the point. If the *painted* plates in Bergman's *Trout* are
the measure of the old order of things, let the lavish *photographs*
of new flies in the *Umpqua Enflycopedia*† stand as the measure
of the new dispensation. The long-argued tensions between
paint and photography in art would, in fact, seem to suggest
similar tensions between the old and the new flies.

The flies of the new *type* have taken on many forms, with a
representative shape or *form* for each of the major aquatic insects:
for mayflies, for caddis flies, for stone flies, and for midges—
nymphs, emergers, and drys. This is to say nothing of the rendi-
tions of countless land insects, crustacea, minnows, even fish eggs
of the stream.

On top of all that, it proved a bold and productive move in
fly fishing clearly to admit the distinction between flies suggesting actual insects and the spectacular *attractor* flies that suggest
who knows what and a little bit of everything—even chunks of
fish flesh. These invaluable patterns, and the principle behind
them, got up their head of steam in the 1950s in the northwest
part of the country and never looked back.

This development has cleared the field for *entomology* of the
actual aquatic insects to move in and claim its essential place in
our angling. We wanted to know *this* mayfly from that one and to
understand the life cycle of the caddis. Where we used to see only
mosquitoes and gnats and maybe an ant, today we can recite, even
in Latin, dozens of midges, a dozen or more mayflies, all the stone
flies, and who knows how many caddis varieties. Hard evidence

that the new angler rejoices in amateur entomology for the fishing day is, again, his fly boxes with, for instance, row upon row of exquisitely arrayed tiny midge larvae patterns. Even we old-timers now have something of a love affair with those insects that trout love. It was the noted Ernest Schwiebert and his *Matching the Hatch* (1950) who produced the first American fly fisher's entomology. He deserves the lion's share of credit for inciting this new and now basic concern of every serious angler.

Nature has come barging into our fly boxes: that's all there is to it. And where we draw the line—or the space in our boxes—between nature and our never-seen-before *attractor* flies is a matter of keenest interest to each of us. We have all of us become *technicians* of the new fly and of the trout stream.

What, then, is the *new fly type* according to the four-part abstract of *form, material, inspiration,* and *use?*

In *form:* the flies are improvisational. No holds are barred. Tyers invent endlessly, but of primary concern is the imitation of trout foods.

In *material:* materials now come from protected environments both wild and commercial and greatly augmented by synthetics.

In *inspiration:* nature, science, and virtuoso tying are the spirit of the thing.

In *use:* the primary use of the new flies is to catch fish, to match the hatch, and to display the craft.

One of the powerful ideas of the last century was that of *Gestalt,* that concept that emerged from the *Bauhaus* in Germany—before Hitler suppressed it. The concept translates out that *form follows function,* that the shape of a thing, its form, depends upon how and for what it's used. This was to become a controlling idea in the new fly tying: *catching fish.*

By the heyday of the Bauhaus in the 1930s, modernism had swept the field in aesthetics and thought, in every walk of life, even sports, for that matter. The pleasant romanticism of our old fishing was fast disappearing in favor of the harder scientific, the pragmatic, the empirical and "technical." The old fixed idea of a fly, dragged along on a heavy gut snell, no longer had any credit.

As noted above, as the new flies moved farther and farther away from the old forms, they tended to use less and less material, to become simpler and simpler, duller and duller (even in their names)—one might say, to become *minimalist.*

I am told and believe that wise trout are to be caught on a small bare hook, sometimes painted, and most likely suggesting a midge larva. This may be as far as minimalism can go. I'm reminded of Samuel Beckett's late plays that distilled the theatrical event down to a bare hook. Where can angler or actors go from here or there?

All this suggests movement beyond the modern toward the *postmodern,* a set of the mind at once more skeptical, suspicious, and analytic yet almost *playful,* certainly debunking, playing alarming variations on themes and the invention of new ones. The postmodern critic, with a blastoff of energy from the counterculture movement of the 1960s, is generally scornful of the past and what is seen as its record of conspiracy on behalf of white, male, straight Europeans—but not so foolish as to disregard it entirely.

Please do read or reread Richard Brautigan's crazy-brilliant little novel Trout Fishing in America *as a wild and compelling way to live in a radically dangerous time and find its meaning in trout fishing. If the author could not survive it, the reader can.*

The postmodern impulse in our lives, almost in spite of itself, has sought appropriate places in art and thought in which to maintain what it treasures from the past. I'm thinking now especially of postmodernism in architecture, where established motifs of the past are recalled not in the engineering of structure, but as *formal ideas, decoration,* and *detail,* often quite playfully, a sort of tribute to the past of which many of us old-timers remain fond.

So, and finally, that question in the title: *Where are the flies of yesteryear?* Unlike the *snows* of yesteryear, we have seen that trout flies responded, like everything else, to historical, cultural, and intellectual pressures and processes of their times, from the romantic to the modern, through wars and rumors of wars, on to the postmodern. The old flies disappeared at streamside, almost forgotten, certainly out of fashion and outmoded for catching trout, but the postmodern idea took them up again and found them a worthy place in our greater angling lives, where they remain as singular objects of art and devotion. They hook us affectionately into our past, where they can be remembered, studied, and treasured in dedicated museums, specimen collections, in frames on walls, in books and luxurious magazines, and in the ritual exercises of memory of those of us old enough to have used them and, when their time came, to give them up.

*The only effort that I know of to study the relative popularity of fly patterns over time as recorded in manufacturers' records of actual sales to anglers is that of Arthur H. Carhart in his nearly forgotten but still valuable *Fresh Water Fishing* (New York: Barnes, 1949). The estimable Carhart published lists of the twelve most purchased flies, first for 1892, then 1935 and 1947. These lists show a marked movement toward the popularity of flies that suggest nature.

†*The Umpqua Enflycopedia* is a complimentary publication of at least 1,000 current flies as developed by leading fly tyers and offered for sale by Umpqua Feather Merchants. Among the 1,000, I could find only about a dozen to represent the old order.

YESTERYEAR? INDEED!

What about that dressing, 1,803 years ago, of the first recorded fly: two waxy colored feathers from under a cock's wattle and red wool that Aelian reported his Macedonian angler to be using for those speckled fish back in AD 200?

Then, over a thousand years later, in 1496, those twelve flies in the *Treatyse of Fysshynge wyth an Angle*?

How about them? That dozen:

The Dun Fly, Another Dun Fly, Stone Fly, Ruddy Fly, Yellow Fly, Black Leaper, Dun Cut, Maure Fly, Tandy Fly, Wasp Fly, Shell Fly, Drake Fly.

This archetypal dozen of flies is described, as we know, in Wynkyn de Worde's second edition of the *Boke of Saint Albans* of 1496. "Described"? Yes, as to their materials or mostly so, but still we don't know what they really looked like, or exactly how they were tied, or even their size.

But fly tying is fly tying wherever and whenever: there are only certain ways that fur and feather can be fastened to a hook. And so we can make informed guesses as how the *Treatyse* flies must have been tied and how they looked. Groundbreaking historian the late John McDonald did the essential research of the matter, and Dwight Webster tied the model flies that have remained most convincing. I imitated those models for my collection of the dozen that I'm admiring at this minute. Grandlooking flies they are. (I am lucky enough to have had a couple pair of hawk primaries that seem to be just the right match for the rolled wings of three of these *Treatyse* flies.)

The twelve flies look just right to anyone who knows flies and fishes them. No wonder they caught fish. One can see why they have so determined the course of the trout fly to this day and how they enjoyed such favor that 150 years later Charles

Cotton could depend on them in his own great collection that was the heart of his contribution to the fifth edition of Walton's *Compleat Angler* in 1676.

It's a dirty shame that it probably was not Dame Juliana Berners, the prioress, who wrote the *Treatyse* and told us of these flies. But we take consolation in the fact that women have subsequently had a profound influence on the invention, tying, and use of flies. Let's remember Mary Orvis Marbury, Carrie Stevens, Helen Shaw, "Fly Rod" Crosby, Mrs. J. R. Richardson, Sara McBride, Chalones Roberts, Megan Boyd, Winnie Dette, Judith Dunham, and the still beautifully kicking Joan Wulff—just to start the list.

Exclusively Flies?
A Reconsideration

IT'S NO NEWS THAT FLY FISHING HAS BECOME *EXCLUSIVIST*. It has, in fact, isolated itself off in a corner of experience away from nourishing contact with the greater tradition of angling, which affirms that from the beginning rod fishing has meant *bait fishing*—fishing with the actual foods fish eat. Only scan the pages of the literature, study the detailed iconography of fishing with bait to learn how sophisticated, rich, and fascinating has been its technology and lore down through the centuries.

We have slighted our history and tradition and given ourselves exclusively to the fly. It is as though the artificial fly now belongs to another order of things, not to the direct appeal to a fish's appetite and need for nourishment. We forget that the fly is merely a substitute for live bait. We forget that the artificial fly came into being only because those small insects on which fish so readily feed were too small to be impaled on a hook, not to mention the difficulty of their capture.* As a matter of practical necessity, then, we had to learn to imitate that form of live bait with an artificial.

When I was a boy, the old-timers would never have called themselves "fly fishermen." They were rather just plain *fishermen* for the working day, ready to cope with any circumstances they encountered, which in outline were live bait and spinners during the early spring season of high and turbulent water, with a natural and unselfconscious switch over to flies as the season settled into midsummer. Such was their time-honored practice.

But several things happened just after World War II that would greatly change things for those old fishermen and make way for us. The advent of spinning seriously dislocated fishing for a decade. Hundred-yard spools of dependable, strong nylon monofilament arrived from France to make spinning practical and revolutionize the sport. Modern transportation made it easier and quicker to fish far and wide. The federal government dammed our rivers and created the tailwaters that are today's big-fish factories. Fly tying suddenly burgeoned in quantity and quality. Wonderfully efficient rods, reels, and lines were everywhere and affordable. Exploding demographics made catch and release an absolute necessity—if there were to be any quality fishing left at all. Fly fishing grew self-contained and *fashionable* into the bargain.

These events combined to develop today's new fly fisherman, who, increasingly isolated, came to scorn the baits of the past that he had never used and little understood.

As one of those remaining few who did fish the old ways, I know the pleasures and fascinations of live bait: worms, minnows, grasshoppers, even, God help me! strips of sucker belly meat. To have commerce with a fish with these baits is a grand experience, at least as demanding of skill and well-regulated tackle as with the fly. To drift a lively angleworm down into a dark hole, to feel a fish begin to work on it, make his repeated attacks, and, after a moment of excruciating suspense, give a steady pull and maybe get himself hooked is keenly exciting. It's an experience that every *complete angler* ought to have. We have our father Walton for authority.

Of course there's a problem—a real dilemma. When we must try to release fish unharmed, the danger of a fish swallowing a baited hook is a serious matter. Though I believe that I can lip-hook four out of five worm-caught fish, I don't want to have to prove it. Releasing fish unharmed from a fly is worrying enough. All of us fail now and then and feel terrible about it.

There is no easy solution to this dilemma. We may take heart in the certainty that few of us will ever give up our singular devotion to the fly. Month in and month out, the most effective way to catch especially trout is with the fly. And it is surely easier to tie or buy flies than to dig worms or seine minnows. Bait, then, is not so much a threat to the fish as *scorning* it and its users is to the character of the exclusivist fly fisher.

If a fly fisher should want to give up the exclusivity of his fly box and reconsider, should he want to return to the bosom of *The Whole and Ancient Company of Anglers* and know the pleasures of live bait, how can he do that without the risk of killing the fish he wants to keep alive and well? It's a dilemma of no mean proportion. Still, I stand on principle and fish a dozen or so worms each season.

But for most, a satisfactory solution of this dilemma may be possible only in the *angler's mind and heart,* in an adjusted attitude, in a *full appreciation* of our complete fishing heritage— and a longing, perhaps, for those simpler days when we could swim a live minnow and creel our fish with pleasure and impunity, knowing that on our side was the justice of the ages.

*The ages-old Irish practice of dapping with live mayflies *(Ephemera danica)* is one exception, and, of course, fishing with live grasshoppers is another grand one.

THOUGHT FOR THE DAY

An angler who cannot feel the pleasure and excitement of a fish's having commerce with a worm and the transmission of that action to a bobber on the surface is fit to die in a ditch and that's all there is to it.
—attributed to Piscator

Toward a Big Six of Great Patterns

Nominations are in order for the half-dozen greatest American trout-fly patterns. We owe it to ourselves to make this determination. I here propose three of them: the Quill Gordon, the Royal Coachman, and the Gray Ghost. I might well have listed the Gray Ghost first and so will open the debate with a few words about that illustrious pattern.

∾

ON JULY 1, 1924, MRS. CARRIE G. STEVENS, a locally well-known fly tyer, of Upper Dam, Rangely Lake, Maine, tied what was perhaps the original and certainly the most influential modern hackle-feather winged streamer fly. It came to be known as the Gray Ghost and made angling history. Mrs. Stevens's inspiration was to imitate the smelt bait fish common in those waters. With her new creation, she promptly went outside to the lake and killed a six-pound, thirteen-ounce brook trout. It and the fly made her famous, a fame that is still growing: witness the many articles, even a major new book* about her.

Mrs. Stevens worked outside the fly-fishing establishment. A few doyens of that establishment knew her personally, while many more knew of her flies and were eager to buy them from her hand. I say "hand" because she did not use a vise, but rather handheld her specially acquired long shank hooks. She said that she had never seen another tyer tie and was entirely self-taught. Her inventions were entirely her own.

In the Matter of Her Gray Ghost

Arriving at an authoritative dressing of the Gray Ghost is difficult but fascinating. Even the spelling *gray* has given me difficulty as I've thought the *e* spelling, *grey*, of greater nuance, better suited to this beautiful and historically important fly. Now, however, I am willing to give in and admit the common and widely accepted *a* spelling. The illustration below is of my own tie.

Mrs. Stevens's celebrated Gray Ghost, 1924.

What can we agree upon as a close-to-the-original, generally accepted dressing? Here's a beginning.

- **Hook:** size 6 to 2; 8x to 10x long shank. (Hooks specially made for the Stevens streamers are now available.)
- **Tail:** none

- **Body:** orange floss, thin
- **Ribbing:** silver tinsel, embossed or flat
- **Throat:** under shank, six or eight peacock herls no more than a half inch longer than the hook. Then sparse white bucktail below herl
- **Wing:** two or four gray (or olive gray) saddle hackles, paired, one-half inch longer than the hook
- **Cheek:** silver pheasant covering the front fourth to a third of the fly with jungle cock on top

That much can usually be agreed upon, but there are complications. I have before me as I write an inferior color photograph, as printed in *Trout* magazine, of Mrs. Stevens's flies mounted for sale on slips of stiff paper and printed with "Made by Mrs. Carrie Stevens, Upper Dam, Maine." I believe that I see on her Gray Ghost a topping of golden pheasant crest. Furthermore, I believe that I see another crest feather as part of the throat, the lowest part, extending back fully one third of the length of the fly. Clearly this model fly employs saddle hackle with blunted, rounded ends for the wing. They ride close above the hook shank and appear to be rather dark gray or iron blue dun.

It is a big fly, a fly to imitate the big smelts that the Rangely brooks preyed upon. It is obviously designed to prevent short strikes and the annoying habit of some streamers to wrap their wing around the hook shank. Very little of the dressing extends back beyond the bend of its very long hook.

I have it on the authority of two writers that the wings of the Gray Ghost are properly tied on the sides of the fly and in Mrs. Stevens's unusual "staggered" method of tying in of wing and throat,* not on the top of the hook as on conventional feather-winged streamers.

Mrs. Stevens came to add a trademark (or hallmark) to each fly she tied—a narrow band of red tying silk wound amidships into the otherwise black head. It's an elegant, subdued vanity that marks a great imagination. We mustn't fail to note that the

Gray Ghost was neither the first nor the last of her inventions or her variations upon the theme of the "ghost." They were several and all of them beautiful.

We should recall, too, that Mrs. Stevens is said to have added or subtracted elements to her original Gray Ghost as she thought they would increase its effectiveness. We are dealing, then, with a fly in process and not an artifact in stasis.

In the several color illustrations of the Gray Ghost on my desk, there is clearly a yellow or golden component. In some there is a long tuft of yellow bucktail under the wing. Jim Deren's dressing shows golden pheasant crest used with the white bucktail under the hook shank as part of the throat. Ray Bergman shows a crest feather used in the lowest level of the wing. George Herter stipulates and shows "yellow polar bear" immediately under the wing hackles.

A Down-East brook-trout fly? A smelt imitation? Alien to the West? Well, yes! But years ago, when I fished the Madison River, down close to West Yellowstone, the rainbows there were highly susceptible to a rather small-sized Gray Ghost when it came swimming down into those gravely basinlike depressions in the river bottom, where they were wont to lie in wait for their dinner. One of those flies from long ago is before me at this moment.

And so, full of enthusiasm for this fly, I close with the proposal that there is no American pattern, the Royal Coachman excepted, with a firmer or more richly deserved right to be listed among the Big Six.

*See Graydon R. and Leslie K. Hilyard, "Carrie Stevens: A Fly Tyer's Progress," *The American Fly Fisher* (spring 2002): passim.

Color It "Isabella"

In his chapter on fly fishing in the fifth edition of Walton's *Compleat Angler,* Charles Cotton describes the Thorn Tree, a good fly for March. He calls for a dubbing of "absolute black with eight or ten hairs of Isabella-coloured mohair."

So, what color is Isabella! No one knew until famed Walton editor Sir Harris Nicholas revealed it to be "a kind of whitish yellow, a little soiled."

Isabella, Infanta of Spain, daughter to Phillip II, accompanied her husband, Archduke Albertus, on his siege of Ostend in 1602, where the good princess vowed not to change her clothes until the city was taken—which took three years. Her linen, as a result, turned out the right color for Cotton's trout fly, whitish yellow, a little soiled.

From Henhouse to Fly Shop

JOHN KLINE, BIBLIOPHILE and retired angling and hunting book dealer, dropped by recently, and with him was his treasured copy of William Blacker's *Blacker's Art of Fly Making, Rewritten and Revised*, London, 1855. I have a photocopy of the 1842 first, rather modest edition and was not prepared for the glories of this 1855 volume with its steel engravings of trout and salmon flies and their tying methods—all brilliantly hand painted. I have a couple of old angling books wherein the steel engravings of flies are hand painted, but they are nothing like these in this Blacker. The colors of the inks and paints here are as fresh and vivid as though applied yesterday and with an accuracy and, I might say, *passion* that bowled me over.

John was trusting enough to leave the book with me briefly, giving me time to read and absorb it all. After I got over the impact of the colored illustrations, I got to thinking about fly tying then and now. How much more intimate, personal, and various it was back then.

Blacker and tyers before and after him, up until nearly our own time, needed to be knowing *naturalists*. They needed to know the beasts of the field and the birds of the air and how to get them to yield up hair, fur, and feather. They "collected" their materials here and there as they could, rather than, as we do now, by driving to a fly shop for them. They combed their spaniels, scraped their hogs, plucked their fowl, sheared their wool, flayed their hares, and hunted everywhere for just the right stuff, even the stuff the local dyer used for his myriad and brilliant colors and shades.

Nothing was synthetic, unless the steel in the handmade hook might be thought a synthetic of iron.... Fur, feather, silk, and steel was the formula, and that was it.

I cannot forget the legendary Theodore Gordon's plaintive request back in about 1890 for a friend to look around in Manhattan uniform shops for the metallic braids that he, Gordon, could then tease out into tinsel for his flies. What if Gordon could walk into one of our superb fly shops of today! What would he think of the array of materials, defying description, in every substance, form, color, texture, and size imaginable—seemingly half of it brilliantly synthetic, even *high tech!*

Yes, the old tyers on both historical sides of William Blacker and his book had to be naturalists—dedicated observers and collectors from the natural world around them. They had to have been more imaginative about their materials. But then, it was easier for them: the barnyard, the henhouse, the pasture and field were everywhere close at hand.

But perhaps the biggest burst of glory in fly tying came with the eighteenth century, "when Britain really ruled the waves." During the Enlightenment and all its excitement, ladies' dress, hats especially, displayed the most exotic, flamboyant plumages of birds from all across the British Empire—and beyond. Style and fashion now extended down into the middle classes and increased the demand for feathers and furs of immense variety and beauty. (Haven't we all always wanted to wear feathers?) How without them could fly tyers have imagined and developed the Imperial Victorian salmon fly that we today so admire and covet, even imitate?

This was the age of the naturalist—professional and amateur—who became important as a collector and classifier, seeking to know and catalog all the world's living things, its entire flora and fauna. Consider the incidental impact of these "scientists" upon fly tying. Their collections and descriptions of birds, mammals, reptiles, and insects were a de facto angler's catalog of possible and now available fly-tying material—fresh from the ships of the sea. Science, fashion, and exploration—naturalist, couturier, and sea captain—became the *angels* of the new fly tying.

Today we are less personal, less *involved* with our fly-tying materials. We are cut off from their sources. We take for granted now that we may own a blue dun cape of undreamed-of excellence by merely driving to the shop. We are dulled to the experience of collecting and dyeing. What was once of *nature* has now become *merchandise.* The fascinating relationship between beast, bird, and the artificial fishing fly is largely forgotten. Instead today we have those lavishly hung peg-board walls of the fly shops dazzling us with everything of which we could possibly dream on the shank of a hook.

What have we to show for this largess, this bounty? Though we are increasingly estranged from the sources in nature of what we tie onto a hook, we are nevertheless in a golden age of fly tying. Theodore Gordon could never have imagined the skill, the invention, and the science that goes into our flies today. Nor could he but have wondered at how our flies take the most difficult fish. We, in turn, well might wonder where we can possibly go from here...?

TAPESTRIES

Any fly tyer lucky enough to have seen the Metropolitan Museum of Art's great exhibition (spring 2002) of late-medieval and Renaissance tapestries should have risked the rebuke of the guards to get his nose up as close to the exquisite tapestries as possible in order to see in detail just what a fly tyer back then might have had to work with.

There are silk threads and flosses in varieties of color and texture to stagger the imagination. There are gilts, tinsels, and cords and flosses beyond count in sizes fine enough for our smallest hooks. And these materials are as fresh in color as when they first hung in great halls and private chambers five hundred years ago.

Certainly an angler of half a millennium ago would have had to scrounge far and wide to fill his dubbing bag with these fabulous stuffs, but they were there. Some tyers doubtless got hold of them directly from the dyers and weavers themselves. These superb craftsmen might well have been as important to our fly tyer of old as the local fly shop is to us today.

Nosing up to these vast scenes in the lives of the nobility, the Bible, and, not infrequently, of sport and examining closely their woven materials restores some perspective on those anglers and their flies back then and on us today. One of the greatest things about the artificial fishing fly is that it is so *elemental* an object and so elemental in its making. It's of the ages—this winding stuff on a hook.

"Oh, We'll Kill the Old Red Rooster When She Comes"
Sung to the Tune of "She'll Be Comin' Round the Mountain"

AS A KID WORKING PART TIME at Tripps Market downtown, I got my particular friend Alan Olson interested in our having my grocer-boss order us a live Rhode Island Red rooster that we could relieve of its hackle. Our hackle in those days didn't amount to much in quality, and this might just be the way for us, in our callow youth, to improve our fly-tying supplies.

I told the boss that we needed a really mature old rooster, which, when he came, turned out to be one hell of a big, tough, mean, and dangerous old bird. I had somehow to get him home, where Alan and I could deal with him. I figured I could lug him tight in my arms out the front door of the store, about fifty yards to the alley where the family car was parked. All the while the old cock, full of malice, was scaring the living tar out of me.

As you might guess, the damned bird gave a sudden powerful lunge out of my arms and onto the sidewalk, where he ran full tilt past the alley and down to the corner, crowing his fool head off. There he turned into our main business street with me in sheer panic right on his tail.

Two or three times I thought I had him trapped in various storefronts only for him to fly at me, spurs and talons in battle array. Of course I flinched, and he escaped, tearing up and down the street, with the good citizens of the town looking on shocked and amazed at the spectacle before them. What was that Wickstrom kid up to now!

Desperate, I threw myself bodily upon my adversary in the doorway of Boulder's posh and finest jewelry store and *had* him, it being a draw as to which of us was the most beaten up.

Somehow I got him back to the car, into a box, and home, where Alan would take charge. He had a "scientific" way to kill the rooster and not bloody the hackle by grabbing the bird from behind, hands under the wings, and crouching with the bird between his thighs. The idea was that pressure from Alan's legs to his hands on the bird's chest would stop his breathing and so suffocate him.

Which Alan did—several times! But that crazy old chicken refused to die. The wretch only *pretended* to be dead by passing out on us, only to come to again and go rampaging all around the backyard. That "backyard" is now covered by this house of ours where I sit writing the history of that great bird's last day.

This grotesque episode in the human comedy ended only after we, as beside ourselves by now as the rooster, just up and took an ax to him.

We skinned out the cape, getting the hackles bloody after all, and discovered, even in our inexperience, that the hackles were worthless—all thick, stiff stems, sparse, soft, webby, overlong barbules of poor, chalky color.

Not even my mother could make the carcass fit to eat!

Orthodox Hackle

When Alan Olson and I were seniors in high school, getting just about old enough to go to war, we were always on the lookout, in our unsophisticated way, for fly-tying materials.

We'd heard that down in Denver, on Market Street, there were two or three kosher poultry-processing firms that would sell the hackle they salvaged from the roosters they killed.

So, off we went to Denver, how, I can't recall and found one of them—processing chickens in the orthodox way, no blood, no scalding water, no mess of any kind, just spotlessly clean ritual skill and lots of crowing chickens. The proprietor welcomed us kids warmly and told us we could have a big paper bag full of loose hackle for twenty-five cents each.

In those days, loose hackle was common in the fly-tying market and was often quite good, depending on the price per ounce. Sometimes it came conveniently sized; for instance, for size 14 to 16 hooks—all neck hackle. I don't remember any saddles and doubt that there were any of any quality at all on those young kosher birds.

Anyway, we were allowed to go upstairs where the chickens, mostly leghorns, Rhode Island Reds, and a few Plymouth Rocks, with a nameless ginger thrown in, were killed by a man we were told was a rabbi. The birds came to him on an endless overhead mechanism, hanging by their feet at his face level. With a small, narrow-bladed knife, the rabbi searched through the chicken's beak and into its brain. The chicken died instantly, going limp and instantly letting go all of its feathers. The pluckers, wearing yarmulkes, followed quickly, close behind the rabbi, and in a solemn rhythm, with three or four fast movements of the hands, stripped the birds completely bare of their plumage.

As a result the floor was deep in feathers, which the workers roughly sorted for their economic value. Neck hackle was separated off, as I remember, along a wall, where Al and I scrambled around on our knees, stuffing our paper bags, even thinking that we would dye the white leghorn hackles all manner of desirable colors. But back home and before too long, we came to realize that this hackle was not very good after all—big, webby, soft, immature stuff, a world away from the superb "genetic" hackles we have today.

At that moment down in Denver, we felt certain that we had struck it rich. In the end, though, what turned out to be most rich about it all—and to this very day—was the marvel of the experience, being allowed a glimpse into an ancient and sacred process of ritual killing, immaculate and humane, ending in

Those Damned Leaders

OUR ULTIMATE CONNECTION TO OUR FLIES is a subtle, sensitive, complex, often stubborn *leader*. Think how we have wrangled over what might be its ideal! How long should it be? How long and heavy in the butt? How fast or gentle a taper? How long and fine the tippet? How stiff or limp the monofilament? What color? Will our ideal leader turn over? Will it drive into the wind? Will the tippet puddle just right for the fly to follow the vagaries of the currents? Will it be strong enough? Will it sink or float? There's a problem for you!

And then think how often after fishing awhile, we have broken off, tangled, and wind knotted our best of leaders until its precise design is long gone. Under fishing pressure we rebuild the front taper as fast as we can, usually without precise calibration or measurement. (My micrometer is too fine an instrument to carry astream and drop on the rocks.)

So, we end up fishing out the day with a leader-extempore and hoping for the best. Our leaders are rarely in their original condition for long. But somehow we soldier on, depending on that almost miraculous sense we have in our muscles of how to adjust our casting to the needs of a modified leader.

The earliest "fly lines" employed no discrete leader at all. Rather, those antique twisted, later braided, horsehair lines (stallion hair, incidentally) progressively reduced the number of hairs in the twist to one or two, at which point the fly was attached.

When early in the eighteenth century silk began to play in the manufacture of fly lines, silkworm *gut* would make possible the modern tapered leader tied up from roughly eighteen-inch strands, each strand drawn out from one of the two silk glands in a silk moth larva and sometimes sized down through diamond dies. When properly soaked, these gut leaders were nearly all an angler could desire and held sway right down into the late 1940s.

My own introduction to leaders was as a six-year-old, when my uncle wanted to take me to Johnson's hatchery to catch a trout. First he sent me over to Valentine's Hardware, telling me only that I was to get "leaders" and that the old men in the store would know what to give me.

I tried to imagine what a "leader" might be and concluded that it had to be some strange mechanical device or other that would lead a worm to a fish. When I was handed three gut leaders in their glassine envelopes, I thought they couldn't amount to much. I had a lot to learn.

Six years later I bought six-foot Japanese gut leaders at Woolworth's at a nickel each, cut them in half, and had two regular three footers for the price of one. I was getting seriously into fishing tackle tinkering.

A technology developed in Japan whereby silk yarns and fluid silk from the worm were combined into "Japanese gut." Leaders made of the best of this material were barely the equal of the poorest of the much more expensive and excellent Spanish silkworm gut.

Then, wonder of wonders, in the mid-1940s nylon mono-filament for leaders and lines appeared and made possible the explosive development of both spinning and fly fishing by radically reducing terminal tackle troubles. But not all of them…

Making or repairing busted-up leaders by joining strands of gut or nylon with the difficult *blood knot* is often frustrating, sometimes ugly, for all but the more practiced of us. Perhaps we are blessed in this difficulty in that it may well keep many rods idling in garages instead of out flailing the increasingly impacted air above our waters.

A DISCOURAGING WORD

My angler's spirits took a sudden and permanent plunge when, long ago, I read an article on drag by an English river keeper. He argued that there's not just one single, generally known film riding the surface of the water, but a horrible *two* films, each slipping and sliding in its own senseless way atop the other and both atop the water itself.

Therefore our dry flies, physically engaged with both these films as well as the principal current, are necessarily yanked every which way and all of them revolting. The forces acting on their drift have become too complex even to imagine.

So, these many years later, when I get what appears to be a beautifully long and drag-free drift of my dry fly, I have to doubt that it's floating free at all. I wish I had never heard of those two films that play such havoc with my floats. I wonder if, in fact, I've ever floated a fly drag free….

Maybe I should have kept my mouth shut about this. On the other hand, this knowledge may be liberating, permitting us to place the blame for our dragging casts squarely where it belongs, on Nature herself—never on our fishing skills.

Fly Book / Fly Box

THE LATE 1930S WITNESSED A DO-OR-DIE STRUGGLE between old leather fly books and increasingly popular fly boxes. The books, with celluloid pages and spring clips or leaves of felt, held snelled wet flies in orderly array. Of course, dry flies always required a box, but sometimes a few might be found squashed between the pages of a fly book.

The question at issue was whether to continue using antiquated six-inch snells on wet flies or to treat them as eyed flies, like dries, and box them.

O. L. Weber, that farseeing founder of the influential Weber Lifelike Fly Company in the 1930s, strongly advocated the exclusive use of eyed flies. Some especially western anglers took offense at the idea that their dear old crusty fly books, full of snelled wet flies and bait hooks, a crushed dry fly or two, spinners, leaders, sinkers, fishing license—any secret oddment— might be a thing of the past.

But it was a losing battle. Snells, awkward and treacherous, lost out. When World War II was won, eyed flies swept the field. The fly book fast became an artifact of angling nostalgia like the split-willow creel.

The revolution, begun by Henry Hall in England in the 1870s, to replace the blind, eyeless hook with a nicely turned-up eyed hook was complete. Today master tyers of specimen flies for display only leap back over the shoulders of Henry Hall and return to the handmade, handheld, blind hook, with a silkworm gut eye loop lashed to the shank in the time-honored way and dazzle us with their skills while stirring up floods of memory.

THE CREEL

Think of the irony in our elevation of the split willow or wicker creel to that of a primary icon of angling. It used to be that nothing, not even the long rod, was as sure a sign of a trout fisherman. Today hundreds of dollars are spent collecting fine old creels— now regarded as objets d'art. Yet were we to see a fisherman wearing one on the stream today, we'd know him to be just one of those outcast fish killers.

The word *creel,* Scottish in origin, denotes generic wicker baskets. In some Scottish villages in the nineteenth century a newly married man was "creeled"; that is, he was required to carry about town a wicker basket full of large stones until the new bride deemed that he might put it down. In the early sixteenth century, Henry VIII made it a "federal" offense to use "creels" to trap smolt salmon.

The legendary firm and final arbiter in all matters of fine fishing tackle, William Mills and Son of New York, offered to the trade in the 1950s its elegant "Beaverkill" model, extra long, narrow, and shallow—just right for three or four sixteen-inch browns to lie full length, beautifully at their ease. What am I offered for mine?

Confessing Heresy

FINALLY, AFTER A LIFETIME OF INTIMIDATION, I screw my courage to the point where I can emerge from the depths of that intimidation and declare my independence from what I believe to be false doctrine: *the doctrine of the cocked dry fly* and "the ideal float line."*

One of the earliest influences on my fly fishing was the Weber Lifelike Fly Company catalog of 1939. The idealized color plates of flies in that luminous catalog set me up for many a frustrating hour trying to match those flies in my Thompson A vise. From that catalog I first picked up the idea that a proper dry fly must ride the surface of the water braced on only the very tips of its hackles and the tips of its tails, its wings straight up and the bend of the hook riding dry just at or above the surface.

Later I learned that this doctrine was propounded by England's great Frederick Halford in the 1880s. Chief spokesman for the dry fly, Halford seemed to insist, amid much pomp and circumstance, that the flies he floated on England's fabled Itchen "cocked" in what I believe is a nearly impossible way. That idea of the cocked fly was reinforced on this side of the Atlantic shortly after 1890 by the equally distinguished Catskill master Theodore Gordon.

Nowhere is the "ideal," I might say, deception, of the cocked dry fly more clearly illustrated than in Art Flick's famous little book, *New Stream Guide*,* wherein the photographic plates show Flick's exquisite Catskill dressings opposite their actual mayfly specimen equivalents. The real mayflies carry their bodies either barely above and almost parallel to the surface on which they rest, or, under full sail, with tails and abdomen reaching upward along that graceful mayfly curve, supporting itself on thorax and legs splayed to front and back.

But Flick's imitations for these naturals, all resting on a *hard surface,* are shown ideally "cocked," according to doctrine, braced between hackle tips and tips of tails, the hook bend and point clearly above the surface. This causes the fly's body to ride thorax and head pointing up roughly at an angle forty-five degrees from the surface, radically different from the natural. We realize in an instant that real mayflies do not "cock" along the "ideal float line," in the Halfordian way.

We know that a needle can float on its long axis supported by surface tension, but that same needle, notwithstanding the matter of balance, cannot be made to float on its point. The point *must* penetrate, and so must hackle points.

Our experience tells us that the hackle tips of our drys will penetrate the surface to a depth where a balanced, natural buoyancy is achieved—when the fly will float. Flotation is achieved when the ruff of hackle penetrates the surface to a depth where an adequate *long-axis length* of hackle fibers *at the sides of the ruff* contacts the surface of the water and takes advantage of *surface tension.* Also, the body will have been lowered toward the surface and rest nearly parallel to it. The tail fibers, like the hackle, will have made long-axis contact with the surface and aid flotation by surface tension with the water's surface "skin." By now, the conventional dry fly is typically resting *high in,* not *on,* the surface.

Our fly will not float "cocked" up on top of the water, like a ballerina en pointe, water being penetrable stuff. Moreover, the rougher the water, the lower toward the surface we can be sure our dry fly will ride.

If we look at properly tied drys of the classical Catskill school, perhaps the most beautiful of all dry flies, we see that the hackle does not (or should not) splay forward and back, that it describes a nearly perfect circular ruff, like an Elizabethan lady's starched lace, of vertically arrayed stiff hackle fibers. Were the hackle allowed to splay toward the eye of the hook and back toward the bend, some degree of horizontal, long-axis contact between hackle and water surface fore and aft would be achieved and so float the fly higher. The narrow, sparse Catskill ruff, beautiful as it is, just cannot but break the surface film like several needles and lower the fly toward that surface.

But and of course, as it sinks deeper through the surface film, bubbles of air are trapped between the hackle fibers. As the fly settles on the surface, these bubbles are packed up closer to the hook shank or thorax of the fly and so help to float it in the manner of a life jacket.

When we false cast, what we achieve in good part is just that replacement of air between fibers, restoring the life jacket, as it were, not depending on the points of the hackle miraculously to support the fly above the surface.

Back in those days when I so suffered the intimidation of the "cocked" dry fly idea, I found myself fishing some superselective brown trout in a tiny alpine lake. Thinking to devise a fly that would satisfy them, I conceived of a dry fly on ultralight wire, with a fullish ruff of the best hackle I could put my hands on, a bit longer than conventional dry fly style—more like a "variant." No wing, no body, just a full, stiff, long tail of the same hackle as the ruff. The tail emerged almost immediately from under the hackle ruff. These minimalist flies came closer to cocking in the Halfordian manner than any in my experience and were quite effective. They worked well, too, on one of England's chalk streams, the river Coln in Gloucestershire. But even these flies, designed in every part for a high float, would subside lower toward the surface in a short time and tend to rest there supported by that air bubble life jacket and the long axis of the prominent tail, which from the trout's point of view might more resemble an abdomen than setae.

I suspect that the development in England of the "variant" form of dry with its longer hackle was a de facto recognition that conventional dressings were too difficult to float as Halford required.

Would not parachute dressings, so popular these days, be yet another recognition of that same fact of life? The parachute splays the hackle to the maximum in order to take fullest advantage of the surface tension support of hackle fibers on their long axis. They may *not* allow as effective a life jacket of air bubbles, however....

Vincent Marinaro went the parachute one better with his "thorax" dun innovation and moved his wing back almost to the center of the hook shank. He then wound his hackle fore and aft of the stem of the wings and hook shank, front to back and back to front, at an angle of roughly forty-five degrees in order to splay the hackle all around and out toward horizontal. This dressing also resulted in a strong life jacket of air bubbles.

Marinaro argued, convincingly to me, that what the trout sees of a mayfly dun is essentially a high-profile wing and body. The insect's legs are of secondary visual importance. The hackle, which may represent those legs, must not impair the trout's view of wing and body. By splaying the hackle fore and aft around the wing, lots of flotation can be achieved along with full exposure of wing and body with the fewest turns of hackle.

Of interest to me is a group of dry flies, engraved in G. A. B. Dewar's important and rare *The Book of the Dry Fly.*† These flies were tied by Mrs. J. R. Richardson of Kingston-on-Thames.‡ All of Mrs. Richardson's dressings employ either hare's ear or *seal fur* for "legs." We all know how effective the traditional Gold

Ribbed Hare's Ear can be, floating, as it does, on its well-picked-out fibers of hair. But seal fur! Well, why not? Especially when one thinks of all the wonderful shades of color it can be dyed. And think of its wiriness, its crinkliness—just like insect legs. When seal or hare is used in place of a conventional hackle, the results are striking, more "natural" than any hackle I've seen. The fur splays out in just the right way to take advantage of surface tension to support the fly on the surface in a most natural way. A bit of underfur left in with the guard hairs tends to hug close to the shank, collecting air bubbles and suggesting a thorax.

This all means to me that a conventional dry fly does not, cannot, float braced on its hackle and the tips of its tail—as though water were the same sort of surface as the tying benches on which we drop our flies from the vise in order to observe how nicely they "cock."

When I look at the plates of English dry flies, nearly all of them show hackles rather soft and splaying out in order both to trap air and to take advantage of as much surface tension on the long axis of the hackle as possible. Even the Halford-style drys allowed their hackles to splay out from a rather full, soft hackle ruff. America's Theodore Gordon suggested that Halford was content with hackle that was too soft. But this softer hackle, well dressed with floatant, may well accommodate itself to the surface and so provide more surface tension than stiffer, web-free, American hackles.

In any case, it was this Halfordian doctrine of the "ideal float line" that discouraged me for so long—until, that is, I ceased to worry about it. Now I have the nerve at last to go into print with such an apparent heresy and risk excommunication from the sainted company of the dry fly: Halford, Marryat, Gordon, La Branche, Steenrod, Darbee, Dette, Cross, Atherton, and Flick.

Truth to tell, though, I feel more comfortable in the theoretical embrace of the likes of that long-forgotten Mrs. Richardson and anything-but-forgotten Vince Marinaro, all those who are willing to admit that their drys float not up above the surface, on an "ideal line," but lower, down on, even in, and parallel to it. Surface tension and air bubbles on the surface film do the work for us, not bracing points of stiff hackle fibers.

Real live mayflies have always known this.

*New York: Crown, 1969.

†London: Lawrence and Bullen Ltd., 1897.

‡Mrs. J. R. Richardson, daughter of Mary Ogden-Smith, was a member of a great English fly-tying and tackle-making company.

That Left Line Hand

One Saturday morning after pancakes, turning on the TV fishing shows for a few minutes, I decided I would keep my eye on the fly fishers' left or "line" hands. I saw what I expected to see, that while we are out there looking out over the tips of our rods to the extension of our casts, looking for fish and strikes, that left hand of ours is living a life all of its own, doing the most subtle and complex operations to make the fishing work.

That line hand is never at rest, always adjusting, constantly masterminding the cast. Yes, it seems to be *thinking*. And do we appreciate it? Not much. We just assume that it will be there doing its essential work.

But I'm forced to admit that sometimes my left hand misses its grab or hold on the line or fouls up in some other way to remind me that it's only mortal, like the rest of me. Sometimes I even get cross with it.

I knew on old fly fisherman on Boulder Creek who didn't have a left hand or even an arm. He used his mouth and teeth instead.

Spinning

GOD, BUT IT WAS GREAT TO GET HOME FOR CHRISTMAS in 1945, to be discharged from the navy and have three hundred dollars mustering-out pay in my pocket. Among other wonderful things to do, there was fishing tackle to get out of storage, pore over, and put to rights in anticipation of May 25, the traditional opening day of the Colorado fishing season.

Life was starting new, I'd gone to war a high school–graduating boy and was now back home, more or less a man. And with a revolution in fishing about to grab me by the throat. It was, of course, the spinning reel or, as our British cousins called it, the "thread-line" reel for the thin light lines that slithered off those fixed spools, sending small bits of hardware to great distances.

The Luxor reel came first from France. The Swiss quickly sent over their Record and Fix reels. The Italians sent perhaps the finest of all a little later in the Alcedo Micron. The English and Scots, who had dominated the manufacture of fly reels for so long, came in last—as far as Americans were concerned—with the Hardy and Young thread-line reels. (The English had already used the term *spinning* for their version of our level-wind bait-casting reels.) Bache-Brown took over Luxor patents in the United States and turned them into the Master Reel. But it remained for the French to dominate the exploding spinning reel market with the famous Mitchell.

Not to be outdone by the Europeans, a Denver angler-inventor, I. V. Humphrey, reconceived the fixed spool reel, putting the spool inside a closed cup on the same axis as the rod, with the crank, as on a fly reel, on the right side. The line issued forth on the left side of the cup from a small hole in the center. Wags called it the "Tin Can." This reel was mounted on a fly rod behind the hand with the boast that the Humphrey required no special rod. This strange reel, which was to have so many later "enclosed spool" imitators, had fatal flaws: it twisted its line, its pickup wasn't dependable, and it didn't multiply its retrieve. In my ignorance—and excitement—I bought and paid for the first Humphrey to go on public sale.

But the European reels, the "coffee grinders," swept the field with serious "spinners." With the spool at the awkward right-angle axis to the rod, these reels had their problems too. The line would often get behind the spool, winding around the shaft in a ruinous way. Nor were they altogether free from line twisting. And the pickup fingers on early reels like the Luxor quickly wore line-cutting grooves. Closed bail pickups were yet to come.

But the real horror of spinning in 1945, the factor that drove us crazy, was the line itself. Our first lines were braided *linen,* which when wet swelled in size atrociously and frayed badly. Then came braided nylon, also soft and twisty and hard to control. Pure misery.

Spinning had to wait, for its full acceptance, for the advent of dependable, regular-diameter, hundred-yard spools of *monofilament* nylon. Of course, we had had nylon monofilament in short strands for our leaders a bit earlier, but we had to wait for the French to send over the first hundred-yard spools under the brand names Tortue and Water Queen. At .008-inch diameter and three-pound test, for instance, they were the salvation of spinning.

By then, most of spinning's woes were in the past. We could chuck quarter-ounce spoons a country mile—if we could *find* those spoons, those tiny bits of hardware. At first, we had to make our own lures or use the big, clunky stuff designed for bass and the level-wind reel.

Again: the French to the rescue! They with the Swiss sent over imaginative and effective little lures just for spinning, not rehashed old bass stuff.

And we began to kill fish. How we did kill them! Our trout had never seen such tempting bits of glittering metal so far out there in the water. They couldn't resist. Both fish and fisherman became the fools of this new technology. We as good as forgot our fly rods and flies and chased after this new love affair—with those stylish light spinning rods of, say, seven feet, with their elegant long slender grips and sliding reel bands that allowed the reel to be placed anywhere along their fourteen inches of cork. The oversized guides, especially the big butt guide with a ring three-quarters of an inch, were fascinating. Ah, the depths, the infamy to which we were seduced!

Seduced into such killing! I recall a moment, almost a rite of passage, when three of us good buddies were cleaning a big mess of fifteen- to sixteen-inch browns we had just taken in a beaver pond–lake in Colorado's North Park. Sitting there, looking over that pile of senselessly dead fish already drying up in the sun, we were shocked at what we had done. Feeling just plain guilty, we promised ourselves never to kill like that again and talked about getting a kit for tagging fish with our own personal tags. (You could get such a thing back then.) Catch-Tag-Release would be our motto. We never followed through on the idea, but our hearts were on the right track.

Spinning enjoyed maybe a full decade during which it was devastating on the fish. "Everybody" got a spinning reel, got the hang of it in a minute, and began throwing lures all over the place. Not a good time for fly fishing. But eventually the fish wised up and began letting our hardware go by without a second glance. The long and the short of it was that many of us returned to our fly rods and found trout still ready and willing to fall for a well-presented fly. We came back to our senses, quit chasing after false gods—or loves, and retired our spinning tackle to fewer and fewer uses.

Now, today, spinning appears to have found its rightful place among our angling technologies and methods. Except, that is, in the persistent practice of some to fish a fly off a spinning reel. The fly gets carried out a hundred or more feet by the infamous "plastic bubble," then dragged over and over, in and out of the water, until some fool trout takes a pass at the trailing fly—a sad way for a fish to go.

But we, who were reconciled with our fly rods after that decade of faithlessness and who took the pledge to quit our wanton killing, took heart in the assurance that the wiliest old trout that swims will always in the end find our right fly, rightly presented, irresistible. Spinning hasn't that necessary finesse.

The earliest image of fishing: Egypt, 2000 bc. From P. E. Newberry,
Beni Hasan, *part 1, plate 29.*

EGYPT, 2000 BC

Above is the world's earliest-known graphic representation of
fishing—from Egypt, circa 2000 BC. Note the use of the rod.
Historian of ancient fishing William Radcliffe puzzles that for rea-
sons unknown, the neighboring Assyrians and Israelites never
employed the rod—only hand lines, nets, and traps.

Radcliffe writes also of the *conservative* character of angling
technology. Not until the seventeenth century in England, after
more than 3,500 years, did the running line appear—as opposed
to a fixed, short line fastened dead off at the rod's tip. A longer line
running down the length of the rod to the angler's hand meant
that a fish could be landed *with* the rod and not the line grabbed
into the hand to pull in the fish. This pivotal development also
made it possible to cast that line in the modern fashion.

Of Cane Poles and Bare Feet
or How One Thing Leads to Another

IT'S ONLY BECAUSE OF THIS SPECIAL RELATIONSHIP that I have with some bass of mine—I say "bass of mine" in the sense that I might have said "friends of mine," were it not that on the whole my friends treat me rather better than those bass.

Those bass live the life of Riley in a pond I'm allowed to fish, from a steep bank sloping some six feet down to the water. These fish often lie right up against the water's rocky edge, their snoots inches away from the shore, one eye on the lookout for crawdads, the other, the evil one, eyeball to eyeball with me. Sometimes I can trick three or four of them by getting on their crawdad side, but usually I'm made a fool of.

So, I got to thinking . . . got to thinking about the old bamboo cane pole of twelve feet with a short line tied dead off the top, maybe as long as the rod. (It's a venerable rig, still used for bream and crappie in the South.)* I wonder if I ought not to try such an outfit, with, say, only five feet of line. With the long pole and short line, I could dap a lure or bait right down on top of one of those all-seeing, all-too-smart bass. I mean *right down exactly on his* *schnoz,* with no line on the water, no disturbance, a big *surprise!* Maybe I could turn the tables and make fools of *them* for a change.

I might need a rubber-elastic connection between pole top and line to absorb sudden shocks—in the British manner, where fishing with cane pole has reached a complexity and refinement of technology to bewilder the American cousin.

Recently I've seen a new English *fishing encyclopedia,*† equally on coarse, game, and sea fishing. This handsome book reveals the marvelous variety of technique and tackle for coarse fishing in the British Isles and Ireland. This quiet, sit-down, slow-to-still-water, highly technical fishing for tench, gudgeon, pike, rudd, barbel, bream, perch, carp, and eel is complex enough to make a trout fly fisherman slink away in disbelief. In any case, I've learned from the British coarse fisherman how better to rig and fish for those bass of mine with a bamboo cane pole.

☙

And that cane pole leads to another thing, away from the techniques of fishing for bass and to the *sociology* of fishing. (For better or worse, there's a sociology of almost everything.)

Think now of that most endearing, if not enduring, icon of American fishing: the barefoot boy, in ragged overalls and straw hat, with cane pole—hook, line, sinker, and bobber—over his shoulder, a can of worms in hand, striding down the lane to the "ole fishing hole."

He's the "country boy" personified—a theme worked and reworked in the romance of America—a dream of the innocent, simple, self-reliant country life, Wordsworthian in its pastoral perfection. He seems caught up in an eternal summer of blue skies, warm sunny days, and fish that never stop biting. He indeed seems to be "trailing clouds of glory" from his origins.

The dream is that this *country boy* will grow up into a proper *country man,* the sturdy yeoman, who, resisting the forces of the city, will always be the source of his nation's strength and character. In him, the Jeffersonian ideal of the self-sufficient agrarian society may live on.

Now here's the sociology. *What*, we may ask, *has become of that country man?* Answer: We all know that *for all practical purposes, he's gone!* The farm boy no longer grows up to replace his father. And with no country men left down on the family farm, there can be no more barefoot boys striding happily down to the old fishing hole. Now, like the family farm itself, it's been sold off to real estate development.

What's left of the family farm has gone *corporate,* and the few sons of the farm who remain beat it as fast as they can, as soon as they can, to the city and life in a Dilbertian cubicle.

Which is not to say that we have forgotten or even given up entirely on country life, but that country life has become largely a *fantasy*—a dream of what the nation must have been back then.

I submit that the upscale, appealing mail-order catalogs have become the gospels and the *lyric poetry* of contemporary faux-pastoral life. The Orvis Company, for instance, lives off the commodification of the myth of "country living," offering its "country" merchandise in clearly lyric terms. We read the descriptions of those highly designed goods as our ancestors read the *Eclogues* of Virgil. L.L. Bean no longer dresses us for the rigors of real Down-East outdoor living, but rather for "casual Fridays" and urban weekends in the countrified international style.

We are tricked into believing that we can live the *immaterial life through material.* When we feel spiritually drained—*stressed out,* they call it—there's always "a month in the country" or two weeks of corporate golf at Vail in which to act out the refreshments of rural life. We're diminished in the process, but it's probably irreversible.

Regardless of how we pretend it might be otherwise, that barefoot boy is no longer among us, except maybe as a presence in a fantasy. His sad demise equals the ever-decreasing numbers of young anglers and hunters. One dare not go barefoot any-place anymore, and traditional low-tech field sports cut little mustard vis-à-vis the seductions of the Internet and its games.

Me? I'm determined to try the cane-pole rig on those bass of mine this summer—and to wonder a little what it must have been like to be young and barefoot.

An Afterword

I did it. I took the cane pole to the pond and found it really taxing to handhold the long pole full length out over the water. It's too heavy and unbalanced and doesn't reach as far as I thought it would. And so life's little disappointments accumulate.

*See the winter 2001 issue of *The American Fly Fisher* for a fascinating article by Andrew Herd, "The Macedonian Fly Revisited." Herd writes on the ancient use of the fixed pole and line on the European continent.

†Tony Miles, Martin Ford, and Peter Gathercole, *The Practical Fishing Encyclopedia: A Comprehensive Guide* (London: Lorenz Books, 1999).

THE GRANGER BAIT-CASTING ROD

I was reminded recently of an obscure corner of western trout fishing that, I believe, had considerably to do with the famed Goodwin Granger rod company of Denver. Granger, in addition to his beautiful fly rods, also built light action, two-piece, six-foot, straight-gripped, cane *bait-casting rods*. And what's more, I knew some who used those rods with the required level-wind bait-casting reels with half-ounce Dardevle-type wobbling spoons. They would wade river, stream, and lake, casting those spoons with their short "plug" rods, bringing up many big trout that otherwise lay too deep and dark to come readily to the fly.

In Arthur Carhart's *Fishing in the West** there are two fascinating photographs of just such fishing on the Little Laramie River. Of course, the advent of spinning made short work of this curious technique.

*New York: Macmillan, 1950.

Propinquity

A GOOD OLD FRIEND BACK DURING MY PENNSYLVANIA SOJOURN told me what I needed to know, that "bass love propinquity." That wonderful word (King Lear made much of it) for closeness, proximity, next-to-ness, whether it be to a certain other person, a deli, a fly shop, an ATM, or, in the case of a bass, a log, a lily pad, a pile of most anything, even a line of shadow. We, all creatures great and small, mostly love propinquity.

"Always fish for bass," my friend said, "up close to anything in the water." The word now in vogue for such stuff is *structure*. Anyhow, I do believe in propinquity in most matters and certainly where bass are concerned.

And now here comes a columnist in *The Denver Post*, telling me more of what I need to realize about brown trout—what I should have articulated for myself—that brown trout also love propinquity. In fact, they can't thrive unless they have stuff in the water or overhead for protection. A biologist for the Colorado Division of Wildlife says that brown trout are "object/cover oriented," a dreary way of putting it compared to the excellence of the word *propinquity*, which says it all.

But it's a serious matter: brown trout, the biologist tells us, cannot increase in "biomass" (a trout-demeaning word) without "object/cover," without something to be close to for security. They need a safe retreat in order to grow much over a foot long. Without proper object/cover, browns cannot attain any size and thrive.

This squares with my experience. Fishing local brown trout waters, I've not seen any increase in the ten-inch average size of the fish. We all know that browns are shy and often in hiding, loving the dark and ganging up in it. And so they're harder to catch, which makes them considerably less desirable to most anglers than the rainbow, for whom water is pretty much water and who are happy to roam wide and free for whatever they can find to eat. The rainbow is the democratic trout par excellence, and his demise is a real political/social as well as sporting problem.

The conventional wisdom I grew up with about browns was that they were fine, even aristocratic fish because they were serious insect feeders and came readily to the surface. Now I see where that sort of wisdom came from—from the East, back when the newly arrived browns were compared with the deeper-feeding, less surface-minded native brook trout, which seemed to be disappearing. It was an antique wisdom that I'd inherited.

Of course we knew of the cannibalistic traits of the brown, how he loved big chucks of meat, like other trout and mice. But still we thought he was the classic trout.

The problem now for us out here in the West is that though the brown is taking over from the whirling-disease-decimated rainbow, he is not thriving in many waters, not increasing in size; in fact, he, like the brook trout out here in the West before him, inclines to stunt and overpopulate. It's a real worry.

What's to be done? Better habitat for browns, of course. But that means *propinquity.* How to find it?

OLD BIGMOUTH

The largemouth black bass must be our ideal catch-and-release fish. Landing him by easily taking hold of the toothless lower lip of his cavernous mouth renders him motionless. We can then easily remove the hook from the paper-thin membrane around the mouth without injuring him. So different from our troubles releasing trout! Furthermore, when sight fishing a hoary old bass, we can get into a real personal, eyeball-to-eyeball relationship with him and as often as not be instructed in the virtue of humility.

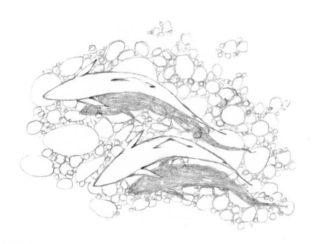

The Brown Trout

WHEN I WAS A KID, THE OLD-TIMERS AROUND HERE commonly spoke of "Loch Leven" trout rather than the German brown, perhaps out of animosity left over from the Great War. Never mind that in Theodore Gordon's day, many called the new *Salmo trutta* from Europe the "yellow trout."

Back then, I could not have described the two varieties, but now I know that the common von Behr brown from the Black Forest of Germany had its red spots and the silver-bodied Scottish Loch Leven did not. I knew then only that a good day with brown trout, whatever their variety, left me with my fingers badly cut up and bleeding from their needle-sharp teeth—and my retinas wonderfully plastered with afterimages of their tail-walking loveliness.

Now, these years later, I've become aware of how superior the Scottish trout was once thought to be. The legendary Charlie Fox, writing from his home on the banks of Pennsylvania's equally legendary Letort, called the *free-rising* Loch Leven the "supertrout." In 1930, 150 of them got stocked into Cedar Run just across the Susquehanna from Harrisburg as a gift from, of all people, then president Herbert Hoover, who planned to come up from Washington to fish them. He failed to appear, but the "Lochs" prospered.

Today, in America at least, the von Behr and the Loch Leven are hopelessly crossbred and their distinction lost to us forever. And so it goes...

But the way it *really* goes is that *Salmo trutta* is once again coming to the rescue. It saved the eastern fisheries from going troutless in the 1880s, when the brook trout was fast disappearing. Now, by virtue of its resistance to whirling disease, this wonderful trout is saving the fisheries of the West! More power to it, teeth and all.

JUST THINK!

Just think, while the brown trout ranged native, with its cousin the Atlantic salmon, over nearly half the northern globe, to say nothing of North American chars, trouts, and northwest salmons, no trout, salmon, or char at all was native to the unlucky Southern Hemisphere.

Had not Europeans insistently taken salmonids to wonderful waters like those in Chile, Argentina, Tasmania, and New Zealand—all points south, where waters swirl in the wrong direction—those lands would have remained bereft of our magnificent northern fish.

Gulls and Guts

IN SPRING WE WENT UP TO BUFFALO BILL RESERVOIR above Cody to fish the mackinaws when they moved in close to shore. It was tricky business working them with live minnows off spinning tackle.

We'd chuck the minnow as far out as we could, let it sink, then wait. If we were in a hotspot, a mac would begin playing with the minnow, picking it up and carrying it toward shore a few feet at a time before dropping it. We'd tighten up on the line and wait for the ritual to be repeated maybe three or four times before the fish did or did not at last slam into it and we did or did not hook him.

We took good messes of two- to three-pound good-eating fish before the work slowed down at noon. Then we'd clean the fish and tie the end of our monofilament spinning line to a gob of guts, sans hook of course, and leave this intestinal rig lying on the shore at water's edge. From there we'd peel off line back up the shore maybe a hundred feet to sit and eat our lunches— and, with rods at the ready, wait.

Wait for a seagull to spot one of those gobs of guts, swoop down, pick it up, and take off. If the gull chose to hang on, we had a real fight on our hands up there in the empyrean over the Absaroka Mountains. I recall that most of the birds gave up the guts rather quickly, but those that were tenacious became a hell of a fight and a threat to our tackle. They might break a rod or clean out a reel.

We laughed because we thought ourselves so very clever having tricked those extremely clever birds. Our justification was that we hadn't hurt, only tricked them, humiliated them.

After all, it was the gull's own decision when to give up his delicacy and fly free. We never "landed" and never touched a one of them.

But our laughter was fundamentally rotten, a cover-up of our embarrassed guilt from so meanly kidding around. What it came down to was our wantonly tormenting those birds—*tormenting* them for fun. Outright killing our fish didn't bother us at all. But deep down we felt bad about what we did to those gulls.

It occurs to me to wonder if today we don't treat our trout much as we treated those gulls back then....

ON HURTING FISH

Just when I thought that I had no more to say about killing fish, about catch and release and all that, when I'd had perhaps more than my fair share of readers' attention on the subject, here come the wild-eyed folks from PETA with proof positive now from British "scientists" that fish do, in fact, feel pain, just as we do. And so, wilder than ever, PETA gets higher up on its high horse and requires that we quit fishing. They are working the argument that catch and release is even more cruel and unforgivable than the outright killing of fish. It's this *pain* business that is fueling their latest intellectual and social distortions—sometimes to the point of violence.

It's interesting how catch and release is now getting occasional blasts of bad press. Me, I've argued that no-kill is regrettable but necessary if we are to sustain trout populations in most of our hard-pressed waters. But I also believe that there is no virtue in it. When we release a fish, we hope unharmed, we are serving strictly our own interests, certainly not the fishes', which we are abusing for our pleasure.

Robert Behnke, as though he any needed authority beyond his own but who, as a fine scientist, is highly fastidious on the matter of authority, draws on vertebrate neurologist Professor James D. Rose to convince me that fish do NOT feel pain. They are neurologically incapable of it. So, when I catch and release a given trout, though I may *injure* it, I do not *hurt* it; that is, I do not make it *hurt*.

The fish certainly experiences the stress of restraint and does what it can to escape—as well it should—but that frantic effort must not be construed as caused by pain. It's bad enough that I put the fish under that stress, let alone recall all those fish of the past that I have injured and either released to die or killed and brought home to eat.

> *One rainbow this spring, whose gills I had caused to bleed,*
> *I had to kill. She was ripe with roe. Not to waste those eggs*
> *utterly, I had Betty sauté them along with the fish itself.*
> *Quite good!*

Professor Behnke makes the case that we ought not to think of fishing as a blood sport or should at least play down that definition. He writes that through the nearly five centuries of record, fishing for trout has been a gentle, contemplative, even, he says, spiritually enhanced sport. Fishing is therefore qualitatively different from land hunting and not a true "blood sport."

> *Behnke, probably the foremost authority on salmonids, also*
> *writes that the Yellowstone River in the park is perhaps the*
> *best proof that catch and release can recover a river in steep*
> *decline. He shows that every cutthroat in the upper river*
> *is caught 9.7 times each season and that the population*
> *sustains itself at that rate!*

For me, there is something skewed in releasing the angler from the accusation of blood because his motivation is of a high order. Is the sport any the less bloody because of our refined intentions?

Me? I want to accept fishing as a blood sport and admit my complicity in that blood. I am complicit in so many evils—think of our world today—and so much blood that the blood I shed out fishing can hardly be noticed. Humans are bloody awful creatures. We are stupid, treacherous, greedy, and violent. But we are also sublime. We have the likes of Mozart on our side to speak for us—maybe even to redeem us.

I argue for both the ancient *rite* and *right* of angling. More and more it's the ancientness of things that stirs me to wonder and action. I accept that I must, in order to live effectively in this world, behave as a modern, contemporary angler, but I do not want to *feel* like one because I fear that is to feel shallowly and casually—if not mechanically.

I want to belong to the old order and believe that the number of people like me is increasing.

I can't recommend highly enough the final chapter of John McPhee's fine new book The Founding Fish* *as a compelling and moving treatment of this complex matter. Also I can't refrain from beating the drums once again for the great Spanish philosopher José Ortega y Gasset's* Meditations on Hunting *as the finest and deepest study of what it means to pursue and kill animals of the hunt.*

I am not a nature lover as such. I do not drive out in the autumn to hear the elk bugle and try to get them on video. I want, rather, to get them on the table—or leave them to the backcountry, where they are unlikely to be "viewed" by every casual driver by.

I believe that nature is often the enemy, a clear and present danger to us all. I do not wish to sentimentalize her or it. Sometimes she or it will surprise me with moments of great beauty and power, but I'm careful to know how to get safely back home.

I am the sort that PETA despises. Their indictments of hunting and fishing, while sometimes almost convincing and sometimes accomplishing some actual good on behalf of animals, their indictments *shall not* trouble my fishing.

I was born a killer and, as a killer, have lived to know the universe through the parallel revelations of Mozart and the Hubble Telescope. I'm convinced that for all our bloodiness, we are the top kids on the block of this universe. We alone have realized and understood the beauty and excellence of trout. Without us, they would be unknown, even to themselves.

Finally, I am convinced, too, that there are more and healthier fish in Boulder Creek today precisely because you and I have fished for them for so long and so faithfully. Where else would those fish have gone for champions as good and true as we?

*New York: Farrar, Straus and Giroux, 2002.

The Other Salmon and MacGuffinism

RECENTLY AT DINNER, OUT OF THE CLEAR BLUE SKY, Betty was scolding me for not including in "the book"* of recent publication (surely you've heard of it) the story of the "other salmon," the American chinook, which preceded rather closely in time those "two Donegal, Irish salmon" that did get their story told in "the book." I defended myself to my accuser, however feebly, with the excuse that I could think of no "MacGuffin" to make the other salmon work as a proper story.

What's a "MacGuffin"? It's that tricky essential device, that turn of things or the *catch* in a story that the great film director Alfred Hitchcock said he needed in order to snap one of his famous films into life and hold it there. A "MacGuffin" is the secret of a story's life.

Now, thinking it over, this *other* American salmon event may have a "MacGuffin" after all, the same one, in fact, as did those salmon in Donegal. And what's more, that same "MacGuffin" might just tie together both salmon stories—of Ireland and of Oregon. Because in both cases my angling success came only after I was bone tired, discouraged, and ready to give up and when in both cases Betty simply would not let me quit. She drove me ruthlessly on to keep after the fish, even when it seemed to me hopeless.

It was in 1956, when the family moved to Oregon for the summer in order for me to join the acting company of the Oregon Shakespeare Festival in Ashland. Fortunately, Ashland is not far from the famed Rogue River and its once great summer runs of chinooks. With one day a week off from rehearsals and performance, I wanted badly to catch my first salmon.

With that single intention, the three of us set off on our Sunday trips. Betty and five-year-old Linnea were willing to spend hours on the banks of the Rogue watching me drift small net bags of fresh salmon roe with my lightish trout spinning tackle: a Record Reel, seven-foot Orvis cane spinning rod and eight-pound French monofilament. It was the same tackle, with the same cast of characters, that in the not-too-distant future would kill those "other" Atlantic salmon, half a world away in Donegal—in Ireland. That's a minor "MacGuffin—" call it *symmetry.*

For three Sundays, I'd gone without a strike, though we frequently saw the great fish moving upriver in all their majesty. At about four in the afternoon of that third and last day of the season, I was more than ready to haul in and go home. Tomorrow would be a hard day of rehearsals and lines to learn. But no! Betty shamed me into going on casting and drifting my eggs. That's what we had come for, and that, by God, was what I was going to do right up to the bitterest end!

So, back into the water I went. Sullenly, resentfully chucking those eggs. Soon, though, only a little later, I could feel that my bait was bumping and drifting just right, down the big, deep riffle. That "pencil" of lead sinker, held to the line by a short length of surgical tubing that would stretch and snap the rig loose from most snags, was bouncing along nicely, enough to move me into a different, excited, and almost magical dimension, able to believe and have faith that I was about to bump a salmon. And I did.

The drifting rig came to a strange and tentative halt, and I came alive. Carefully I began taking up line against what I hoped was a good fish. Coming gently up tight and feeling *life*, I let the fish have line with which to move off slowly across and down-river, probably looking for a place in the gravel to rebury those precious loose eggs that had no business floating free that way—or so said the old-timers.

What, then, was there for me to do but lean back and drive home the treble hook hidden in the bag of roe! The battle was engaged: the obviously big fish trying hard to break me off, banging its head on the rocks but staying within reasonable range. I tried to play it smart and stylish—as though I knew what I were doing.

People began gathering to watch the show, the first of what would become my gallery—my audience—of a couple dozen anglers and passersby, several of whom generously offered their advice as to how to fight the fish. I nodded gratefully and ignored them.

When I'd been into the heavily dogging fish for maybe fifteen minutes, it decided to take off fast downriver, arcing clear of the water seven times. All I could do was hold on and hope that the drag on the Record's spool—for which the brand was famous—would do its sensitive best.

Following the fish for most of a hundred yards, I soon was forced ashore to make my stand, do or die. Directly across the river, on a high jutting of rock, were three fishermen still-fishing out into the current where my fish could be expected to run. Miraculously it had passed them by on its heroic jumping run downriver without fouling in their lines.

Down there, at the bottom of the long, long run, my salmon mercifully decided to stop and slowly, grudgingly, allowed me to begin pumping it back up the current. By now the gallery was getting really excited. Daughter Linnea was dissolved in tears, sure that her dad would lose his fish. Betty was feeling smug and vindicated. Another fisherman ran for his gaff, just in case. Somebody lit me a cigarette. (Those were *those* days.)

My gallery, fearing that the guys still-fishing across from us would foul my fish, began yelling at them, reminding them of the established courtesy of the river that one pulled in so that a hooked fish might be fairly fought. The gallery had become a band of loyal supporters, partisans.

In good time, the men across the way handsomely reeled in and all was well. My salmon, at the end of an hour of hard, slogging work, was, at last, pumped back up the current and into slack water at my feet, where it stayed down deep and wouldn't come up.

The fellow who had run for his gaff now threw himself on his belly, his arm and gaff thrust into the water to his shoulder, and made frantic passes at the deep-down fish—scaring me to death. I had images of his hitting the line with the gaff and breaking off the fish.

But the gods were with me. I convinced my helper that he must wait until I could at last raise the fish, which I did and at which time he drove the gaff home and brought the fish to ground. Twenty-five pounds on the mark, forty inches, a bright, fat, beautiful, fresh-from-the-salt chinook that turned out to be a *she*—a *she* that left me dazed with pride and pleasure.

After photos, congratulations from one and all, Linnea's tears turned to happy smiles, and Betty now quite, shall I say, *self*-satisfied, it was back home to Ashland, where I cut the fish into steaks that made for the finest eating of the summer. But first, we saved all the little scraps of flesh and meat from the head, which Betty fried, sort of scrambled, for breakfast next morning. That was the best ever.

The Oregon Shakespeare Festival made PR hay, its own "MacGuffined" story, of their crazy actor who was out after salmon on his every day off. Come to think of it, maybe that's yet another minor "MacGuffin" of mine because in an interesting way it was Shakespeare, his performance and study, who made it possible for me to go after these fish—in Oregon and, twenty months later, in Ireland. But the big trick of the story, the *essential* "MacGuffin," is that relentless woman who wouldn't let me stop fishing and drove me on. To this day she gloats over both stories and considers herself their heroine.

*Gordon M. Wickstrom, *Notes from an Old Fly Book* (Boulder: University Press of Colorado, 2001).

AE, YEATS, AND SYNGE

I'll bet that there are few fishers of the fly who can boast that they have a drawing of all three subjects of their Ph.D. dissertations sitting in the same boat, fishing flies. They are those leading figures in Irish drama and literature: William Butler Yeats, AE (George Russell), and John Millington Synge, doing just that on their dear friend and likewise leader in the Irish Renaissance Lady Augusta Gregory's wonderful and magical Coole Lake near Galway.

Irish literature was never more than a pen point away from images of salmon and trout—images in which those fish are always more than just fish.

Hickories and Herrings

ENOUGH ABOUT SALMON! After all, there's the *shad,* a fine, fine fish—fine to look at, fine to fish for, and maybe even finer to eat. And nothing derivative about it, no European counterpart for precedent, truly all-American, the American shad!

The American or white shad, *Alosa sapidissima,* like the salmon, pastures at sea and returns from the Atlantic* to spawn in fresh water beginning in late November in Florida, then, week by week, enters yet another more northerly river up the east coast until the annual run is completed in Canada in June.

In the olden days, east-coast rivers were choked with shad. Our forefathers harvested them in huge numbers—from the Susquehanna, for instance, often with pitchforks by the buckboard load.

Though the flesh of the shad is delicious at table, the female's roe is the more sought after as among the most delectable of dishes. The only drawback is that the shad is a holy terror of intricate bones, nearly impossible to eat around unless you know what you are doing. The old-timers along the eastern seaboard developed a method of baking a shad on a plank so slowly—over hours—that the bones (most of them) simply melted away. But it was a tricky process, hard to time just right. We never succeeded at it in our household.

Otherwise one must have one's shad *boned* by classically skilled eastern fishmongers—efficiently, though in ritual secrecy. I've often seen shad being boned in the market—or rather *not* seen it, because the boner invariably put his body between me and the fish he was working on. I was not supposed to know how to do for myself what for him had the status of privilege, that of a guild craft.

But oh, my! when he finished, those beautiful slabs of white fish! Nicely broiled with a set of roe alongside, with spring asparagus . . . and a decent white wine! I can hardly bear to write about it.

I've never caught an American shad myself, though; never even fished them. But I have fished for the smaller *hickory* shad, *Alosa mediocris*. Instead of the three to five or six pounds of the whites, the hickories are on average a pound and a half to two pounds—fifteen to eighteen inches. They have a nice habit of preferring streams over the big rivers and so, with their great fighting characteristics, make for terrific fishing—best in the cool of an early morning or evening when light is low. I've worked over them in April—when it's said they come with the blossoming dogwoods—in Maryland's Octoraro Creek, a tributary of the great Susquehanna, which, of course, flows into the even greater Chesapeake Bay.

Coming upstream on their brief runs, they like to hang for a while just over and above the lip of a pool, in water of moderate depth, there to slash at simple, though weighted, brightly colored flies swinging past them. They hit hard and immediately throw themselves into the air in the most beautiful jumps and are a hard fight. Often when one locates a mess of them, they can seem to hit almost every cast. At other times, though one knows that they are there, right under the fly, they can be mysteriously difficult to move. My friend Dick Henry of Lebanon, Pennsylvania, almost as experienced with shad as with difficult brown trout, puts it this way:

There is a certain touch, or sense, to hickory fishing that I once had but now have lost. My quartering casts with four mends catch fish but not the way they did years ago. I've never known a more complex fish to try to understand.
I won't even mention the various fly patterns and fishing techniques that work so well for some, because none of it makes sense.†

Nevertheless, once a hickory is in hand or net, he or she must be carefully caressed to see if the belly be fat and stuffed enough to qualify as a roe (female) fish. To the roe-hungry angler, a disappointing few seem to qualify. Most turn out to be bucks, while many a hen's roe isn't yet ripe enough to give her that swollen belly that tells the angler what he's got—male or female. So the fish get returned to the water. Few anglers will take bucks home because, if the bigger American shad is a creature of multitudinous bones, the hickory seems only more so, what with the same bone structure concentrated in a smaller and therefore more impossible-to-eat-around package.

In our household, we figure we can eat most anything and everything, and if we kill it, we feel obligated to eat it. But on one trip, a couple of these hickory critters that I thought might just be roe or hen fish and so provide the wonderful eggs turned out, when opened, to be bucks after all and beyond even my wife's ability to make edible—rather like those (and fortunately they were few) tough old Wyoming sage chickens, those old bombers I mistakenly brought down and so had to bring home to try to eat. (Sometimes the gravy wasn't too bad.) We may conclude, therefore, that hickory shad, though not much for the table, are certainly *something* for sport!

To stand there halfway down a big pool or run, to the knees in the water, and sling those bright flies quartering down to those fish who come smashing at them and then, like silver bullets, try to blow the place apart—fish after fish! That's what I mean.

Once when slugging it out with the hickories in Octoraro Creek on an April morning, for some reason I happened to look back over my shoulder and lo! there behind me, in six inches of water, was a brilliant, shimmering silver-blue mass of eight- or nine-inch fish—herring!—going hell-bent upstream. I'd never seen a live herring before, though I've never seen the *dead* herring that I didn't love and love to eat, having grown up on them in their Christmastime pickled condition and, as a kipper, in many "full" English breakfasts. And first cousins to the shad they are too.

So, I turned quickly around, away from the shad, to cast almost at my feet to the myriad racing herring in their blur of silver-blue. They were moving too impossibly fast for them even to think of hitting my fly. Still, one odd fish, out on the edge of the school, held back a bit and decided to turn on my fly and I had him—and had him home to pickle and eat! I had caught myself a herring! One of the great fish, *the wheat of the sea*— once so plentiful, important, and emblematic, especially in northern European economies and culture.

I literally didn't know which way to turn that day, to the hickories or to the herrings. It was a great day in the morning, for sure.

---

*In 1871, the great fish culturalist Seth Green sent shad fry to California, where they were released into the Sacramento River. The transplant was a great success. Good runs of shad are found all up and down the Pacific coast. Nevertheless, Californians, besotted as they long have been with their dwindling salmon and steelhead, have failed fully to appreciate the excellence of shad both as sport and cuisine.

The standard work on shad and fishing them has been C. Boyd Pfeiffer's *Shad Fishing* (Harrisburg, Pa.: Stackpole Press, 1975). John McPhee's new *The Founding Fish* may well be the last, best, and most elegant word on these truly American fish.

†Hurricane Agnes of 1972 effectively wiped out the hickory shad in its mid-eastern range. It was commonly thought that they were gone forever. But the good news is that recent springs have seen the nearly miraculous return of the hickories out of nowhere and in good numbers.

UNCLE THAD ON THE DELICACY OF SHAD

Has it ever occurred to you, sir, when you eat a pair
of fried shad-roes for breakfast, how many shad you
consume in embryo? If the roe is from a good-sized fish,
certainly not less than twenty-five thousand. O thou
piscivorous Leviathan! thou has devoured in germ,
at a single meal, and merely as a relish to thy coffee,
a hundred thousand pounds of fish.... But quiet thy
conscience, gentle monster, for with all the chances
of hatching, and the dangers to which the shadlings
are exposed, it is doubtful if the eggs thou hast
swallowed would have produced more than two or
three four-pound shad at the end of three years.
—Thaddeus Norris, known among anglers
as Uncle Thad and perhaps the greatest figure
in early American angling, in Lippincott's
Magazine, 1869

For a definitive discussion of preparing shad roe, milt, and the flesh of this superb fish for the table, see John McPhee's "Sapidissima: The Most Savory Fish," in his *The Founding Fish*. No one writes on shad—or much of anything else—better than McPhee.

The Natural Corral

I

NORTH OF CODY AND WEST OF POWELL, a slab of the Big Horn Basin tips upward toward the Absaroka Mountains. Back in the 1950s, in that bad old last century, an old dirt road switchbacked its way up the long, seemingly featureless slope toward Dead Indian Hill before dropping into the valley of The Clarks Fork on its way out of Wyoming and on to the northeast corner of Yellowstone. It was and still is, though now tamed by a fine new highway, tough, superb country.

But back then, we weren't going all the way into Montana. We knew of some fine fishing in a hidden canyon lost to view back on the Wyoming side, on that ascending plain. Somehow or other, we knew on which of those nearly identical switchbacks to pull off and gear up for the hike down into the Natural Corral.

First we had to sidle north a quarter mile across the rocky slope—to a point where the earth suddenly fell away at our feet into a sharp-edged ravine that began not far above us as no more than a scratch in the dirt and grew rapidly into a draw, then to a gulch, to a gully, and to a ravine, where we stood, and, by this declension, on down to become a little canyon.

Any passing stranger back on the road, seeing us working our way across the side hill, must, at the instant we started down into the ravine, have thought that the earth suddenly opened and swallowed us.

189

A hard-going sort of trail angled down into the bottom of the ravine. In some places we could hardly keep our feet, but then it would widen out for a few yards into something suggesting an old wagon road. We puzzled over that.

There was no sign, other than that trace of what might have been a road, that humans had been there before. Still, the air felt thick with the resonance of lives of the long-gone cattlemen who had once used this secret place, not like us moderns to fish but to make a living off their herds. I felt rather like an intruder.

The bottom of the ravine, at first only a few yards across, was a whole new world from the rocky grasslands above. The dry little streambed made a smooth and easy sandy trail down toward the corral. Hemmed in tight by the vertical rimrock cliffs, the flat bottomland held a bit of moisture of its own and showed all the variety of flora and geology of a great western canyon in miniature— but totally private, utterly quiet, secret and intimate.

II

The canyon floor steadily widened, increasing in scale and majesty as we walked the comfortable trail, steadily downward, toward our fishing. As the ravine turned more into a canyon, we gave in to ghost fantasies of the old West. We felt privileged to be there—but on our good behavior.

But the crucial thing is . . . in maybe half a mile the deepening canyon pinched itself off against its north wall, threatening a complete blockage—but for a narrow defile, a passage through the rock, wide enough for a single horse or a couple of us anglers to pass. Had there been water in the bottom, it too would have had to flow through this singular narrow cleft before suddenly flowing out into the wonder of the Natural Corral itself.

To step through that rock defile out into the vast bowl of the Natural Corral . . . well, it's stunning. In retrospect it recalls every such experience of which we have ever dreamed, of passing from one world into a greater Other. Recall with me how, in mountain country just like this, the mortally wounded gunman Lassiter saves Jane Withersteen in Zane Grey's *Riders of the Purple Sage*. Think how at the end, the hotly pursuing really bad men from town want to capture Jane and force her into sexual and economic submission. Remember how they chase her and Lassiter deep into the mountains and how the heroic Lassiter helps her up and through Deception Pass, their own secret crevice through which to crawl to safety—but never to return. By rolling the great stone into the narrow defile, their safety becomes their total isolation from the world: it becomes their love/death in the Hidden Valley of peace and plenty on the Other Side. Think, too, of that Himalayan mountain trail passing through just such a gap in the mountain wall where suddenly Shangri-la, the ultimate refuge, appears before the desperate climbers in all its dreamlike beauty—in *Lost Horizon*. It's a universal dream of life, an archetype of our inner experience of ourselves; the archetype, though I hate to write it right out loud, of birth itself. It's exactly with that sort of power and magic and meaning that the Natural Corral, consciously or not, strikes us on our first sight and experience of it.

Passing through that narrow gap in the canyon wall (how many times we have seen its like in the movies!), we are struck silent at the sight of the dark stratifications of the rimrocking cliffs suddenly curving outward like great caliper arms reaching around to embrace a rich, verdant meadowland bowl of two small lakes, beaver dams, copses of aspen and willow—most of a thousand yards across. To the east, the bowl opens out, with cliffs falling away to disappear into the flatland valley below, clearing an unbroken and magnificent vista of the Big Horn Basin stretching away to the far horizon. Up that almost impassible eastern lip of the corral there was said to be a dangerous and tortuous trail coming from the ranch land below. Tales tell of rustlers driving stolen cattle up that trail and into the secrecy of the corral—the perfect hideaway for bandits.

Sixty years before I first looked out of the corral at the vastness of the Big Horn Basin, Buffalo Bill had looked out on that same great desert and imagined how with water it could become a new American Garden of Eden. I didn't know back then, half a century ago, as I set up my tackle against this immense backdrop, that it was the great man's vision that opened up this land to the likes of me, where I could have a home and family and a life as a teacher of kids, teaching them what had been done with language and what they could do with it, especially when they spoke it in plays from the stage. But I know it now, even as I know truly about the life and times of Wm. Frederick Cody. I know it as I sit here rigging the tackle of this essay and feeling profoundly fortunate.

III

But this is an essay in a book about fishing—or supposed to be. The thoughts of a fisherman are hard to confine and often tend to stray: he tends to get contemplative as the hypnotic rhythm of the cast takes over. So then, about those beaver dams above the lakes! They drove me crazy on that first trip. Terrible, impossible tangles of willow protecting five-pound rainbows that I could hook and fight but never land. They loved any big dry fly and tore the place apart with them. But sad to say, they disappeared completely after that first year's encounter. A mystery.

The crowning jewel of the place, though, was the upper, the biggest and deepest of the two lakes—a beautiful oval, maybe an acre, an idyllic, spring-fed little mountain lake. In the northern corner, if an oval can have a corner, was a spectacular underwater spring gushing up, from about fifteen feet down, into a broad bed of white sand. This purest of water ceaselessly rolled and roiled this purest of sand in an extravagance of aquamarine beauty. It was maybe twenty feet across, always with a dozen or so good-sized trout swimming or rather drifting, as though dreaming, on the spring's invisible currents—perfect silhouettes serenely floating in the space of water.

No one could resist casting to them, but I never got more than a lazy nod of the head for my pains. At the edges of the sand, I could sometimes get a strike, but even that was tough.

Out on the lake proper there were many brook trout, ten inches to a foot long and mostly willing. Among those brooks were a number of rainbows of two to three pounds, the yellowest rainbows I've seen, not as willing as the brooks but not impossible either.

In those days I was learning all I could about nymphs and fishing them and was under the influence of John Atherton's *The Fly and the Fish* (1950) and his appealing theory of impressionism in fly patterns and design. I tied his nymphs with carefully selected colors and tints of dubbing, and the Natural Corral fish loved them. In that ultraclear water, I could see nearly every move a trout made to my fly and so had an ideal laboratory in which to practice the craft of the nymph.

Those were the days when we killed fish, but the thought of lugging a heavy creel or gunnysack of fish back up the relentlessly ascending trail out of the corral was a real consideration: one of those big rainbows would be quite enough. Other than that pleasant worry of a too-heavy creel to lug home—with all the other tackle, including waders that we thought we could not do without—there were the rattlesnakes sunning themselves on rocks at the lake's edge. This place was surely an Eden in its own right and mythic detail.

And there was the occasional lion or deer and soaring eagles. On one trip in, I recall being paced by a considerable lion on the rimrocks overhead. The big cat seemed only casually interested in us before disappearing into the rocks. It was, for us, a peaceable kingdom.

IV

At the close of this essay and of this book, I want to hike back up through memory, out of the corral, to that cleft, that gap, in the canyon wall and take time to look back on the extraordinary scene. I want to get my hands on its stony sides and push—as though holding them apart—and think more on what the place evokes.

Zane Grey's Lassiter and Jane are a model of the situation. At their heroic moment, at Jane's powerful urging: "Roll the stone, Lassiter! Roll the stone!" with the last of his energy, he rolled it, thundering down into the gap, sealing them off forever from the outside world. We imagine them turning away from the blocked-up Deception Pass toward a kind of primitive perfection from which there can be no return, where there is no society, no economy, no industry, no arts and sciences—and no need of them. There was, as I said earlier, only their love and their death trapped together in that Happy Valley. And so it is with so many of the stories about slipping through a great gap out of this bad world into another where all is blessing, every need provided for, where everything is forever safe and secure. The "corral" into which the lovers go is a complete and closed system. The world outside? It no longer exists.

But here I am now, standing in this rock cleft, pressing its sides apart as though to keep it open, looking back down into the great bowl and beyond over its far and impassable rim to where I must return on Monday morning, to that school to teach those kids something about living their lives out in the great world. That means I've got to turn around, pass through the cleft, and get up that trail, back up around the way I came, up and out of here, and back to work.

Come to think of it, much of life may be thought of as a slipping through a gap, a tight spot, out into a larger arena of possibility—or of danger and defeat.

It's not as though you and I are inexperienced or unpracticed in this. All of us have been slipping through gaps of one kind or another from the beginning. If it is an archetype of birth, it is also one of death. At the *very* end, we no longer look back to our daily work and prepare to return. There's ultimately that Big Gap through which to pass to...we know not what, and quite beyond our comprehension.

I'm certain that it's no Happy Valley, no happy hunting ground of perfect fishing. But I do suspect that it's a kind of perfection in its own right: the perfection of *nothingness.*

In my effort to wrangle with this, I think how King Lear in his folly snarled at his daughter Cordelia, "Nothing will come of nothing." He was dead wrong. Everything comes from nothing, especially that *absolute nothing* out of which came our matchless planet and our matchless human lives—with all our living loves, our deaths, and even our fishing.

So, may it not be possible that the Big Secret, which we alone in all this astonishing universe are here to grasp, is that we all must slip through that ultimate gap, out into that perfect and infinite *nothingness* that is really the ground of all being and the potential for everything?

In any event, going down into the Natural Corral was always an extraordinary occasion. It gathered us into a rough magic of fine fishing and a landscape of mystery. It could even suggest a sustaining idea about the nature of things—which is often the best thing about going fishing in the first place.

Nice to have met you out on this stream of words.
You take good care of yourself.
I'm going home.